Labor Mobility
and
Economic Opportunity

Labor Mobility and Economic Opportunity

Essays by

E. WIGHT BAKKE

PHILIP M. HAUSER

GLADYS L. PALMER

CHARLES A. MYERS

DALE YODER

CLARK KERR

Preface by
PAUL WEBBINK

THE M.I.T. PRESS
Massachusetts Institute of Technology
Cambridge, Massachusetts

HD
5724
L12

Preface

*Vice President, Social
Science Research Council*

This volume is a co-operative venture to make generally available the results of intensive research and thought over many years at half a dozen leading university research centers. The conceptual and statistical analysis of the major general attributes of labor mobility by Philip M. Hauser, based upon his work at the University of Chicago and earlier in the U. S. Bureau of the Census, provides an effective background for the interpretation of the subsequent essays. The principal findings of a series of pioneering studies undertaken at the University of Pennsylvania, the Massachusetts Institute of Technology, and the University of Minnesota are presented by Gladys L. Palmer, Charles A. Myers, and Dale Yoder. Impediments to labor mobility are discussed by Clark Kerr in his chapter on "The Balkanization of Labor Markets," and important interpretations of certain crucial problems relating to the future flexibility of the American economy are given in Miss Palmer's essay on "Social Values in Labor Mobility." These considerations, and others, are summarized in challenging fashion by E. Wight Bakke in the essay that introduces the entire volume.

The suggestion that this volume be prepared grew out of the research planning discussions of the Committee on Labor Market Research of the Social Science Research Council. The authors are members of this Committee, which has been concerned for some years with the identification and encouragement of basic research on the behavior of labor markets. Particularly intensive efforts have been directed by the Committee to the analysis of the factors affecting occupational, industrial, and geographic mobility in individual labor markets and for specific groups in the labor supply. In the course of these efforts the Committee has sponsored a major study of patterns and factors in labor mobility in six cities and a technical appraisal of research developments relating to labor mobility, both of which will be published by the Social Science Research Council during the present year. These undertakings and other related research have been subjected to thorough review and criticism at sundry research conferences held under the Committee's auspices, and these discussions have in turn been reflected in the research of the Committee's own members and their associates. It seems timely, therefore, to bring together the results of certain of their studies and of their current thinking as a progress report on this significant phase of labor and industrial relations research.

The members of the Committee are convinced that a special responsibility for assuring the additive character of research rests upon research workers who have succeeded in establishing relative continuity of their research activities. All too often findings are published in separate reports and monographs, each concerned solely with the results of a particular project. A considerable accumulation of information, experience, and tentative conclusions tends to remain sequestered in the minds of individual research workers. The Committee holds, therefore, that research workers should periodically summarize their accumulated findings and relate them to the work of others. It hopes that the present volume will represent a step in that direction and will stimulate others to undertake still more rigorous work, so that the scientific basis for judgment and prediction concerning labor market and labor supply problems will be extended.

PAUL WEBBINK

July, 1954

Contents

1. Introduction

E. WIGHT BAKKE

Sterling Professor of
Economics and Director of
The Labor and Management
Center, Yale University

This introduction is not written for economists. Among them, interest in labor mobility and movement is traditional. The concept of
labor mobility has long been a significant component of their model of
the dynamic reality of economic operations and of the growth of economic institutions.

It is written for the man who, seeing this title, may think, "Here is
another one of those academic discussions among economists of a
matter relevant only to their own trade." Nothing could be farther
from the truth.

To be sure, the reader will note that the essays in this book are
written by economists. He will find that one essay explicitly sets forth
a number of consequences of its generalizations about labor markets
for traditional economic theory, and that such consequences are im-
plicit in all the essays. He may observe that the name of the Committee of the Social Science Research Council (Labor Market), which
sponsors the volume, sounds like a chapter title from an economic
textbook. He may recall from his courses in economics that "labor
mobility" is paired with "mobility of capital," and that, in economic
theory, both are supposed to result when the owners and buyers of
these "commodities" seek some economic advantage for themselves.
He may recall that economists use the concept of labor mobility when
they theorize about "relating the supply of to the demand for labor,"
"optimum allocation of resources," "wage determination," "manpower
mobilization," and other problems whose labels reflect the professional
language of the labelers.

But if he infers from these observations that labor mobility is of
no interest to him or concern of his, as an ordinary citizen, he will miss
a very important fact. In exploring the realities of labor mobility and
movement the economists are studying a factor which has important

1

effects on the stability and progress of our form of economic, social, and political life, and which can help or hinder every individual in our society in his attempts fully to realize and express his ambitions and abilities.

Economists may have started to work on the problem of "labor mobility" in order to perfect their models and theory. As scientists they could not miss the important impact of the movement of workers from one job, or employer, or skill, or locality to another on the development and adaptation of economic techniques and facilities. Nor as scientists could they rest easy with assumptions made about how and why this movement took place. They wanted to test those assumptions and reduce the amount of guesswork in such an important matter by going into the field and learning from firsthand observation how people in a labor market behave, how they get assigned to or choose different jobs and skills, how much change and flexibility there is under different circumstances or at different periods of time.

As the essays in this book indicate, however, when they explore the realities of human behavior associated with the problem, they find themselves not only introduced to matters which vitally concern the development of an economy which will provide the population with an increasing quantity and quality of material goods, and with the tactical and strategic decisions which add to or subtract from this development. They find themselves also concerned with a process whose results have a mighty impact on the kinds of noneconomic institutions we have, the psychology and habits of individuals, and even the development or decay of the central values that individuals in our culture seek to realize through those institutions. This does not make their initial theoretical and practical problem any less important. It makes it more significant by relating it to a broader universe of human experience and interest. Since this introduction is written for the noneconomist, it is the relevance of labor mobility to this broader universe which will be emphasized.

Several of the authors have suggested that the free choices of individuals as to where and for whom they will labor and of employers as to whom they will hire are essential features distinguishing a business from the previous forms of societal organization. It is sometimes argued that the technological possibilities given to us by the industrial revolution might have been used to great material advantage, even if men and their families had been ordered about like slaves from one job to another, and owners and managers had been required to accept their "allotments" of man power from an economic dictator. No one acquainted with the facts believes that. The free movement of labor is in large part responsible for the flexibility with which millions of people and an amazing number and variety of jobs have been matched, for the vast potential of enterprise, initiative, incentive, invention, and for the self-development and acquisition of skills, which contributed greatly to our economic development.

Of equal importance, moreover, is the contribution of freedom of labor movement to the development of the typical familial, political, religious, educational, and other social institutions characterizing Western society. Had these institutions developed to satisfy the life needs of a working population whose movement was severely controlled, had they not been subject to acceptance and rejection, and to the critical and creative efforts, of men and women whose opportunity for place and type of livelihood was subject to individual choice, their contributions would have been far less vital. Certainly they would have been different.

Even more important is the fact that the faith in, and reliance upon, the individual, so central to the development of democratic life, could not have outlived its brave declaration, unless individuals could choose to a high degree, as employers or employees, those with whom they would associate themselves. Whatever may be true of the few who inherit a superior social status, the achievement of an increasingly satisfactory social status by the many *through their own efforts* is geared to the freedom with which they may choose the place for, and type of, "making a living." And the full achievement of any organizer or manager of a business or industry is handicapped to the degree that he does not have free choice in deciding who will work for him and who will not. When we speak of "free" or "voluntary" movement of labor we mean that stimulated by *private* decisions, whether those decisions are made by employers or by potential or actual employees.

Had the Marxists given appropriate attention to the human initiative, inventiveness, and adaptive skill unleashed by freedom of labor movement, they would have been less confident of the internal decay of a "business civilization." Had they taken due account of the normal reaction of individuals to an economic system which promised them an individual status toward which they could move by making choices as to how and where they would make a living, the Marxists would not have been so puzzled by the "dumbness" of workers who resist involvement in the "class" struggle.

It is, of course, true that the freedom of this movement of labor varies in degree among different occupational, industrial, and social groups. It varies from that stage in the business cycle when jobs are plentiful to that stage when they are scarce. It varies between the unstructured and the highly structured labor markets. The difference is marked as between Europeans and Americans. It varies from normal times to those of threatening emergencies. But the differences, and their consequences for the adaptability and productiveness of the groups involved, only emphasize the central importance of the factor whose variation is indicated.

When economists study labor mobility and movement as a vitalizing and adapting factor in the organization and operation of our economic methods and tools, they are exploring something in which we all have a deep concern. Even if we want or need to interfere with that process (movement of workers), as is often the case, it is important that such interference be carried out by people who know what they are doing and what they are really interfering with.

The occasions upon which regulation of the flow of labor to jobs and away from jobs appeared necessary have multiplied since 1930. Even, however, if wars were unknown, even if the need for mobilizing all resources, including manpower, to the limit never became pressing, even if economic activity had never swung from high to low as it has in successive business cycles, we would be concerned with having enough flexibility among the people who work to meet the normal opportunities for and problems of change and growth in an economy, its social institutions, and its people.

Yet, whether our concern is stimulated by an emergency or by interest in long-run development, it is even more necessary today than in the past for us to examine our assumptions about how and why our resources of manpower get associated with the need for manpower. This is the area of national interest in which economists, like those writing in this book, are working.

The investigations of particular labor markets concerned with what types of, how, under what circumstances, and in response to what incentives workers moved from one occupation, industry, and geographical area to another are not, therefore, just studies suggesting to economists necessary revisions in their "wage" or "allocation of resources" theories. They are reports of findings derived from studies as to how and why we were able to operate and grow in strength as a national economy without regimenting our people into jobs that they had not chosen voluntarily as likely to promote their individual interests.

Moreover, the results of such investigations, some of which are reported in this book, raise the insistent question, "Can we, in the face of a short-run emergency, depend on the same stimuli which moved men from one job to another in the past to be effective in getting the kind and quality of human productive effort we need at the moment?" None of the authors of these essays answers that question. But they do suggest to policymakers and administrators the realistic factors that have motivated or compelled men to move in the past.

Another fact of current American history which stimulates the interest of economists in the matter of labor mobility is this: Reliance on free movement of laboring individuals has costs as well as benefits. We have not yet recovered as a nation of people from the impression left by the depression of the thirties. The decline in opportunities for employment was so marked in that period that the most reactionary defender of our economic system could scarcely exclaim, "In this period, any good man can get a job." We were forced to consider, as an important factor in the "free" choice by workers, this question, "What opportunities for work are 'freely' offered?"

All our economic assumptions about rational and free choice among job opportunities went by the board as we surveyed the experience of unemployed workers looking for "any port in a storm."

In this period of full employment, we are inclined to erase from our memories the facts of that period, but the experience has left its mark on our thought. We cannot ignore the fact that demand for, as well as supply of, labor is a factor in arranging the allocation of a labor force. As every one of the authors of essays in this book has indicated, the motivations and skills of the potential labor force must be coupled with the demand which appeals to those motivations and utilizes those skills.

Moreover, we have found that institutional adjustments have been made to the costs of free mobility which alter the character of our problem. Union-management agreements build fences around job territories and limit the people who may offer to do work in those territories. Seniority provisions in union contracts, pension plans, both private and public, devices such as vacations, promotion schemes, and profit sharing, dependent on length of service, and other devices have increased the equity of particular workers in their present jobs and have, consequently, reduced the possibility of movement and the incentive to move.

As economists, we could, of course, take refuge in that peaceful harbor of the scientific mind, "all other things remaining equal." But some scientists, including the authors of essays in this book, refuse such sanctuary.

As economists and responsible citizens, therefore, we are faced with these facts:

1. Free movement of labor is an essential foundation stone for our kind of society.

2. The utilization of that principle of action has been an important, if not a controlling, factor in the development of our present economic, political, and social institutions, the opportunity for improvement of individual status and expression, in short, of our way of living.

3. Once established, that way of living engenders habits associated with, and stabilities in, career, family, and community activity, and in thrift and foresight techniques, which restrict the spontaneous job movement and mobility of people, at the same time that they provide the certainties and security so essential to satisfactory and effective life and work.

4. Some degree of flexibility in the movement of labor is essential both to maintain the stability and effectiveness of economic operations, ways of living, and individual action, to make it possible for institutions and people to adapt to changing opportunities and problems, and to provide for growth and development of people and the social facilities essential to their living.

5. The necessity for maximum utilization of all our resources in recent years has forced us to ask more insistently than in the past whether our method of free movement of labor based on employer and worker choices directed toward individual advantage can be retained as a basic procedure for manpower allocation.

6. To this point in our history we have not had to answer that question with facts. On the whole we observed the results and found them satisfying. A categorical "Yes," based on faith and evangelistic fervor, was enough.

7. In the interest of both long-range and immediate economic, political, and social effectiveness and growth, we turn with deepened concern to this question: Can we gather the facts about why, when, and how people move jobwise, under the circumstances of life in our society in our time, that will enable us to organize our human resources by persuasion rather than by compulsion, and to strengthen our economy without destroying the chief distinctive contribution that we have to make to a developing industrial and business civilization?

8. In short, can we undergird the economic and social strength of our nation by adequately and efficiently distributing our labor re-

sources, without destroying, for the human units of those resources, both workers and employers, the free choice and free movement which, as assumed rights, have encouraged them to loyalty to the American system?

It is an easy inference, from the observation that economists are studying those factors which encourage and discourage the movement of labor, that they are handmaidens of those who would *manipulate* that movement for particular purposes. To be sure their findings may be so utilized. But nothing in the conclusions set forth in these essays would encourage economic or political leaders to suggest manpower allocation devices which *compelled* reluctant or resentful compliance rather than *elicited* enthusiastic co-operation.

The sponsors of this book, the Committee on the Labor Market Research of the Social Science Research Council, invite your attention to the publication not merely because it contains some findings and comments of people who are devoting their professional careers to recording and analyzing the empirical facts of labor mobility and movement. We solicit your attention because the problem with which these authors are concerned is central to our survival as a nation dedicated to the principle that that group is economically and socially strongest, most secure, and most able to contribute to civilized life, which *elicits* the energies of *all* its people, not just of a chosen few. Free choice by the worker as to the area of production or services to which he will devote his energies and free choice by the employer as to whom he will employ are essential principles upon which the past performance of this nation of people is based. Let us consider carefully, therefore, as these authors do, how those principles have worked out in practice, and what implications for present and future policy are revealed in the recorded facts.

2. Mobility in Labor Force Participation

PHILIP M. HAUSER

Professor of Sociology
University of Chicago

Labor mobility in respect to labor force participation is a relatively recent phenomenon in human history. As a concept it is applicable to a mass population only in our modern urban industrial society. Consideration of changes in a population of "workers," as distinguished from changes in the population in general, presupposes a society in which "work" is differentiated from other activities such as play, education, worship, or courtship. In a preindustrial folk type of society in which work is not sharply differentiated from other life activities, it is not possible to consider entrance to, or exit from, a working population. Our culture, however, embodies sharp distinctions among various activities including the designation of "work" for those contributing to the production of goods or services.

In the development of our society, productive activities have been increasingly detached from the other activities of life for the large bulk of our population. "Work" consists, in the main, of the performance of specific tasks in the production of goods or services, usually in a specific place, during specified intervals of time, and under an agreed-upon set of conditions. In general, in our society, it is easy to determine when a person is, or is not, "at work." To be sure, however, a number of marginal activities are not so clear-cut.

Not all persons who "work" in the sense defined above are uniformly regarded as members of the working population or, to use the current designation in the United States, of "the labor force." Moreover, some persons are regarded as being in the labor force even though they are doing no work. Those who are seeking work, that is, who are "unemployed," are also part of the population of workers. Our current practice of counting or analyzing "the labor force" includes specified categories of those who "work" and those who are "seeking work."

8

"Work" which identifies a person with the labor force consists in the main of those activities which contribute to the production of goods or services for the market. The work of housewives, or of unpaid family members working less than 15 hours per week on farms or in family business enterprises, even though productive of goods and services, does not place the person in "the labor force." Similarly, the work of inmates of institutions such as prisons, workhouses, homes for the aged, and the like, or the work of persons under 14 years of age, is not regarded as "labor force" activities. On the other hand, persons without work experience who are seeking their first jobs, or persons with previous work experience who have no job connection but who are seeking work, are regarded as members of the labor force in our current practices in the United States.[1]

Different countries in the world have varying conventions on the inclusion or exclusion of various categories of workers in their "working populations."[2] Variations in practice are found especially for "marginal" categories of workers such as housewives, unpaid family workers, youth, and the aged. For example, France defines all farmers' wives as in the labor force, whereas Sweden excludes them categorically. In the Philippine Census of 1939 women doing housework were combined with domestic servants and included in the "active population"; in Mexico, in 1940, both housewives and servants were excluded. In the United States we exclude housewives but include domestic servants. In Czechoslovakia domestic servants in the homes of their employers were excluded from the labor force—others were included. In Canada, in 1941, "new workers" were excluded from the working population, whereas in the United States they were included.

The conceptual framework and methods of measurement used to analyze the size and composition of the working population definitely affect the results obtained.

Two general approaches to the study of a nation's productive manpower have evolved in the experience of the Western World. The first, and most widely used for census purposes, is the gainful-worker approach; the second, originated in the United States during the late thirties and used for the first time in a national census in 1940, is the labor-force approach.[3]

[1] See Bureau of the Census, "Census Bureau Measurement of Unemployment," *Labor Force Memorandum 3*, Washington, June 25, 1948.

[2] See United Nations, "The Labor Force: Problems of Census Definition and Enumeration," *Studies of Census Methods, 4*, New York, April 1948.

[3] Louis J. Ducoff and Margaret J. Hagood, *Labor Force Definition and Meas-*

In brief, the gainful-worker approach hinges around the return of an occupation by a respondent to an enumerator, does not have a clear-cut time referent, and involves the person's conception of his status rather than his activity. Under this approach the working population, or gainful workers, includes all those persons who have reported a gainful occupation; and excludes all persons who have not. The labor-force approach may be described as an attempt to obtain a better approximation of the labor supply as conceived by the economist. It includes as in the labor force all persons who report that they have actually worked at any time during a specified period—the week preceding the census or survey; or who report that they were actively seeking work during the same period. Although the labor-force concept is based essentially on an activity approach and is tied down to a definite time referent, these principles have been compromised in dealing with marginal cases. Thus the person with a job but not actually at work during the week is included in the labor force under specified conditions; and a person not actually at work nor actively seeking work may also be included under certain conditions. The complexity of our employee-employer nexus is such that it has been necessary to recognize inactive categories of both persons at work and persons seeking work.

In principle, the labor-force is to be preferred to the gainful-worker approach when it is desired to study changes in the working population as an approximation of the labor supply over relatively short intervals of time. The labor-force approach is used in the United States, for example, to measure monthly changes in size and composition, and in Canada to measure quarterly changes. The definite time reference and, in the main, activity basis for response in the labor-force approach provide a better series of observations than does the gainful-worker approach for the analysis of the dynamics of a working population.

Each of these approaches—the gainful-worker and the labor-force—has its usefulness, and both, depending on national circumstances, are recommended for use by the I.L.O. and by the United Nations.[4] The size and composition of a working population, however, vary some-

urement, Social Science Research Council, Bulletin 56, New York, 1947; Philip M. Hauser, "The Labor Force and Gainful Workers—Concept Measurement and Comparability," *American Journal of Sociology,* 54 (Jan. 1949), 338–355.

[4] United Nations, *Population Census Methods,* New York, 1949, Chapter X; International Labor Office, *International Standards for Statistics of Employment, Unemployment, and the Labor Force,* Montreal, 1947.

what, and significantly, for certain categories such as new workers or retired workers, depending on the framework actually used.

The concepts of work and of a working population are then products of a given culture—of our own urbanized and industrial culture. Moreover, within the urbanized and industrial part of the world, attempts to count or describe the working population involve the use of more or less arbitrary frames of reference and methods of measurement. With any given set of concepts and measurement methods, however, it is possible to study the working population in either its static or dynamic aspects. This essay is concerned with various considerations relating to movement into and out of the labor force as this concept is used in current census and survey practice in the United States.

TYPES OF MOBILITY

Movement into and out of the labor force frames all other forms of labor mobility. That is, all other forms of labor mobility—changes in job, employer, occupation, industry, place of work, or combinations of these changes—may be regarded as changes occurring within the framework of change in labor force participation itself. Similarly, changes in status within the labor force—changes in employment or unemployment or various subcategories of these statuses—occur within the framework of changes in the total labor force. Since changes in the size and composition of the total labor force are bound to affect these other forms of labor mobility it is essential, in the interest of maintaining perspective, to gain an understanding of the dynamics of labor force participation, of its relative flexibility or rigidity, of its patterns, and of the factors associated with its changes.

The study of changes in labor force participation may be pursued in a number of ways.[5] A paradigm may be constructed for analysis in at least three dimensions. First, changes in labor force participation may be analyzed in terms of the usual concepts of time series analysis —secular, cyclical, seasonal, and other changes. Second, each of these types of changes may be analyzed into its components of change—into gross as well as net changes. Third, each of the changes, gross and net, may be further analyzed in terms of the factors associated with or producing the change, and these may be classified in several ways,

---

[5] This essay is concerned with mobility in labor force participation of persons as units rather than with labor input. Consideration of changes in labor input could, however, on the whole, follow the same pattern.

among which one classification of factors might be economic, demographic, cultural, political, social-psychological or personal, and "all
other." This paradigm may be presented in conceptual tabular form
as a three-dimensional table.

PARADIGM FOR STUDY OF MOBILITY IN LABOR FORCE PARTICIPATION

Types of Change	Factors in Changes in Labor Force Participation					
	Economic	Demographic	Cultural	Political	Personal	"All Other"
Total						
Ins						
Outs						
Secular						
Ins						
Outs						
Cyclical						
Ins						
Outs						
Seasonal						
Ins						
Outs						
Other						
Ins						
Outs						

Moreover, this paradigm may be followed in respect to two other
elements of analysis—space and the family as a labor force unit. That
is, the analysis of changes in labor force participation may be conducted for specific geographic localities and their interrelationships;
and the unit of analysis could be (and should be) families as well as
individual workers. Finally, the analysis could be conducted in terms
of the total labor force or any of its components by sex, age, color,
nativity, or other characteristics.

Let us turn next to a consideration of each of the elements of this
paradigm with special attention to the types of knowledge we have
or are in process of acquiring and the gaps in, and limitations of, the
data prerequisite to an analysis of the kind proposed.

SECULAR CHANGES

Data exist for at least a rough analysis of long-run changes in labor
force participation in the United States and in a number of foreign
countries. These are in the form of census statistics which have in-

TABLE 1.   LABOR FORCE PARTICIPATION RATES OF PERSONS OF WORKING AGE,
UNITED STATES, 1870–1950

Percentage of Persons of Working Age in the Working Population

	Gainful Workers 10 yr and over [1]	Gainful Workers 14 yr and over [2]	Labor Force 14 yr and over [3]
1950	....	....	56.8
1940	....	....	54.1
1930	49.5	54.5	54.6
1920	51.3	55.6	55.8
1910	52.2	57.9	....
1900	50.2	55.0	....
1890	49.2	....	....
1880	47.3	....	....
1870	44.4	....	....

[1] Taken from A. M. Edwards, *Comparative Occupation Statistics for the United States, 1870–1940*, Bureau of the Census, Washington, Government Printing Office, 1943, p. 90.   Data are adjusted for comparability.

[2] Taken from Bureau of the Census, "Population and Labor Force Trends in the United States," *Current Population Reports*, Series P-45, No. 11, Dec. 1945. Data are not adjusted for comparability.   The data for 1920, particularly, are not comparable because of acknowledged relative overcount.

[3] Taken from Bureau of the Census, "A Projected Growth of the Labor Force in the United States under Conditions of High Employment," *Current Population Reports*, Series P-50, No. 42, Dec. 1952, p. 8.   Data are adjusted for comparability with current labor force data.

cluded in addition to the usual run of demographic data information about the working population as obtained through either the gainful-worker or the labor-force approach.

Such analyses as are available for the United States and other Western countries show a great stability in the over-all labor force participation rate.   Restricting ourselves to the United States, the data show that, since 1870, the first date from which time series analysis is possible with some accuracy, the proportion of the total population of working age in the labor force has changed very little.   This conclusion is justified no matter which of the competing sets of data, raw or adjusted, are used.[6]   Table 1 contains a summarization of the proportion

[6] The Bureau of the Census has published various series of data adjusted and unadjusted.   Selected series of these "official" data are shown in Table 1.   For the most detailed private estimates and adjustments see John Durand, *The Labor Force in the United States, 1890 to 1960*, Social Science Research Council, New York, 1948, Appendix A, pp. 191–218; and Clarence Long, *Labor Force, Income, and Employment*, National Bureau of Economic Research, 1950 (volume available to writer in mimeographed form).

TABLE 2.   GAINFUL WORKER PARTICIPATION RATES BY SEX AND AGE, UNITED STATES, 1890–1930

Percentage of Persons Who Were Gainful Workers, for Specified Sex and Age Groups

Year and Sex	10 yr and over	10–15 yr	16–44 yr	45–64 yr	65 yr and over
Male					
1930	76.2	6.4	89.2	94.1	58.3
1920	79.9	16.8	93.1	93.9	60.2
1910	80.8	21.7	93.3	92.1	63.7
1900	80.0	26.1	91.8	93.4	68.4
1890	79.3	25.9	90.6	95.2	73.8
Female					
1930	22.0	2.9	29.7	18.7	8.0
1920	21.4	5.8	28.2	17.1	8.0
1910	21.5	8.1	27.8	16.2	8.9
1900	18.8	10.2	23.5	14.1	9.1
1890	17.4	10.0	21.7	12.6	8.3

Source: A. M. Edwards, *loc. cit.* (see Table 1).

TABLE 3.   LABOR FORCE PARTICIPATION RATES BY SEX AND AGE, UNITED STATES, 1920–1950

Percentage of Persons in Labor Force for Specified Sex and Age Groups

Sex and Year	14 yr and over	14–19 yr	20–24 yr	25–34 yr	35–44 yr	45–54 yr	55–64 yr	65 yr and over
Male								
1950	82.4	47.5	86.9	94.4	96.5	94.6	85.1	45.0
1940	80.9	38.4	89.2	96.3	96.6	93.7	85.6	43.3
1930	83.4	43.5	89.6	96.5	96.9	94.8	87.6	55.5
1920	85.9	55.9	90.7	96.2	96.6	94.5	87.4	57.1
Female								
1950	31.9	26.4	44.4	33.5	38.0	36.9	27.3	9.5
1940	27.4	19.9	47.8	35.3	29.2	24.2	17.8	6.7
1930	25.1	23.8	43.9	28.7	23.3	21.3	16.4	8.2
1920	24.1	29.6	39.3	25.0	20.6	19.4	15.3	8.2

Source: Bureau of the Census, *loc. cit.* (see note 3, Table 1).

of persons of working age in the labor force as published by the Bureau of the Census.

Having in mind the basic social and economic changes which took place in the United States between 1870 and 1950, the rapid growth in total population, and the major changes in the composition of population, it seems little short of remarkable that the labor force participation rate remained so stable throughout this period. The relative rigidity of the total labor force participation rate, however, obscures important gross changes in the participation of various subgroupings of the population by age and by sex.

Varying estimates are available on the proportion of the population who were workers by sex and by age. These variations in estimates also arise from the differences in adjustments made in the raw census data.[7] Again the official data of the Bureau of the Census are shown in Tables 2 and 3.

These data, in summary form, portray the secular decline in the work participation of children and of oldsters, and the considerable increase in the labor force participation of women.

The proportion of males in the middle ages in the labor force changed but little, however, over the years. Males 25 to 64 years of age may, in fact, be regarded as the central core of the labor force and show little mobility in respect to labor force participation over time.

These gross changes [8] of opposite direction in labor force participation have during the past eighty years or so largely offset each other. In consequence the net change in the proportion of persons of working age in the labor force has been relatively small.

Although much remains to be done in the way of research into the factors associated with the secular changes in labor force participation, some studies are available which at least highlight some aspects of the problem.[9]

[7] Durand, *loc. cit.*; Long, *loc. cit.*

[8] These "gross" changes in respect to the net change represented by the total labor force participation rate are, of course, "net" changes in respect to such considerations as "ins" and "outs" of specific subclasses of the categories. Analysis of "gross" and "net" change is possible at any number of levels, depending on the refinement of the data available.

[9] Sanford Dornbusch, *The Family in the Labor Force*, unpublished Ph.D. dissertation, University of Chicago, 1952; Paul Douglas, *The Theory of Wages*, The Macmillan Co., New York, 1934; Paul Douglas and Enka Schoenberg, "Studies in the Supply Curve of Workers," . . . *Journal of Political Economy*, 45, Feb. 1937, pp. 45–79; John Durand, *op. cit.*; Alba M. Edwards, *Comparative Occupation Statistics for the United States, 1870–1940*, Washington, Government Printing Office, 1943; A. J. Jaffe and C. D. Stewart, *Manpower Resources and Utilization*, John

Edwards has pointed out the important effects on the labor force of our changing economy—especially in the decreased demand for workers in agriculture and the increased demand for workers in white collar and service pursuits. Palmer and Ratner have analyzed some of the implications for labor force participation, particularly of women, of our changing industrial and occupational structure and their interrelationships. Long has dwelt particularly on the effects of changes in income level and wage structure on labor supply and has also summarized some of the relevant economic literature. Durand and Jaffe and Stewart have dealt with the effects of a number of economic factors on the changing labor force, and with a number of cultural factors as well, including the changing role of women, increased educational requirements and exposure, the changing role of oldsters, changes in family composition, and various other changes, such as marital status, urban-rural and rural-nonfarm residence, color, nativity, etc. Durand and Wolfbein and Jaffe have analyzed in some detail the effects of demographic changes.

The generalizations that can be drawn on the secular changes which have occurred in the labor force leave much to be desired. The data permit a reasonably good description of the size and composition of the labor force over the last 60 to 90 years, but they are far from satisfactory in explaining the "why's" of the changes or the mechanisms through which they occurred.

Wolfbein and Jaffe after standardizing the population for various factors conclude in their analysis of labor force participation rates between 1890 and 1930 that "social and economic forces are much more important than measurable demographic factors in accounting for changes in the proportion of the population in the labor force."[10]

Wiley & Sons, New York, 1951; Clarence D. Long, *op. cit.,* also "The Labor Force and Economic Changes" in Richard A. Lester and Joseph Shister, *Insights into Labor Issues,* The Macmillan Co., New York, 1948; "Labor Force in Wartime America," *Occasional Paper 14, National Bureau of Economic Research,* 1944; Wilbert Moore, *Industrialization and Labor,* Cornell University Press, Ithaca, 1951; Charles Myers and George T. Schultz, *The Dynamics of the Labor Market,* Prentice-Hall, New York, 1951; Gladys L. Palmer and Ann Ratner, *Industrial and Occupational Trend in National Employment, Research Report 11,* Industrial Research Department, University of Pennsylvania, 1949; Gladys L. Palmer, *Labor Mobility in Six Cities,* forthcoming volume; Herbert Parnes, *Research in Labor Mobility,* forthcoming volume, Social Science Research Council; Lloyd G. Reynolds, *The Structure of Labor Market,* Harper, New York, 1951; S. L. Wolfbein and A. J. Jaffe, "Demographic Factors in Labor Force Growth," *American Sociological Review, XI,* 4, Aug. 1946.
[10] S. L. Wolfbein and A. J. Jaffe, *op. cit.,* p. 396.

Durand has shown, in somewhat greater detail, the effects of demographic changes on the labor force and has included a broader range of factors in his analysis. He has concluded,[11] "Taken together, demographic factors are a fairly important part of the explanation of the past rise in the ratio of the labor force to the total population, the reduction in labor force participation of males, and the increase of the female labor force. In the future these same demographic factors can be expected to continue their influence upon long-range labor force trends, acting on the whole in much the same way that they have acted in the past." Long, in focusing primarily on the relationship between the size of the labor force and changing income levels, reinforces earlier conclusions on the inverse correlation between income and the labor force participation rate, at a given time, especially for the marginal workers, that is, women and young persons; but he found no evidence of a similar relationship over time. On the basis of his rather laborious studies, Long has set forth a number of generalizations about the labor force but many of them, as he recognizes, are of a tenuous character. Particularly relevant at this point is his "first law of the labor supply," which he states as follows: "The labor force of any area or country, standardized for changes in the size and structure of the population, remains at the same level in short or long run regardless of increases or decreases in worker income." [12] Despite his skillful marshaling of data, this generalization is at best acceptable as a working hypothesis rather than as a law. Long is to be commended for his assiduous efforts to substitute research with empirical data for the easy theorizing of some economists about labor market activities. But, unfortunately, the data are not yet adequate to provide a basis for the definitive testing of the critical hypothesis involved.

It is clear that in the United States and in other Western countries, there has been a downward secular trend in the labor force participation of young persons and of older persons. It is also clear that there has been a marked secular trend upward in the labor force participation of women and, particularly, in that of married women. It is true that these conflicting trends have tended to cancel one another so that the proportion of persons of working age within the labor force has remained relatively stable. Such data, however, available for the United States and a few other countries, hardly justify firm generalization at this time. All the data may be regarded as representing samples drawn from Western countries in approximately the same state of the

[11] *Op. cit.*, p. 83.
[12] *Labor Force, Income, and Employment*, Chapter 12, p. 1 (mimeographed).

"demographic revolution" and industrialization. The total labor force participation rate is the net effect not only of changing specific rates by age and sex but also of other basic changes, social and economic, including shifts in urban-rural residence, declining fertility and mortality rates, an aging population, fluctuating marriage rates, changes in retirement practices, increase in and prolonged school attendance, changing size of family, changing role of women, increased productivity, decreased hours of work, increased real income, technological changes, and changing provisions for various forms of security.

The question, "How do we account for the relative stability of the labor force participation rate of persons of working age?" is a most tantalizing one in the circumstances. But in the present state of data and knowledge the answers can only be speculatory. On the whole, the literature on factors accounting for labor force changes, except for the effects of demographic changes, may be more aptly described as suggestive rather than definitive and has done little more than pose the basic problems involved for more intensive investigation.

In terms of our paradigm large gaps exist in the data for assaying the influence of most of the economic, cultural, political, and personal factors in labor force participation. To be sure, classical and neoclassical economic theory sets a frame for understanding certain aspects of the labor supply, especially in "the long run." But empirical study, thus far, has not been able to provide an adequate test of the general theory, nor has it produced definitive findings on many specific hypotheses.

Much more work also remains to be done on the influence of our changing culture on labor force participation. Such generalizations as have been drawn on the effects of the changing role of women, decreasing family size, social stratification, urbanization, and the like have been largely of a speculative rather than of a research character. The effects of our changing political scene on labor force participation, particularly as manifested by the "bloodless revolution" of the "New" and "Fair Deals," have hardly been mentioned, as yet, in the literature, much less investigated. It may, in fact, be too early to judge its effects. But it would seem that such changes as those represented by the Social Security System, various elements of the agricultural programs, labor legislation, and the large number of specific enactments and measures and general political climate tended to change the pattern of income distribution. This might well have influenced the pattern of labor force participation.

Perhaps the greatest gap in our knowledge is that relating to the "personal" factors in labor force participation.[13] Within the framework of broad economic and social forces which undoubtedly determine the total labor supply in our society, there is a wide area of personal choice in entering and leaving the labor force—at least for workers other than the hard core of males 25 to 64 years of age. There is need for basic research into the "personal" factors in labor force participation—that is, in social-psychological research into such problems as motivation and personal and family decisions.

On the whole, data on the working population and on related factors are still too fragmentary and unsatisfactory to permit definitive analysis of the type proposed. It is possible and desirable, however, to focus on research in this area. And it is of considerable importance to build new and more satisfactory data which will make possible more fruitful researches in the future. In this connection the efforts of the U. S. Bureau of the Census to provide more detailed tabulations of statistics on the labor force in the decennial censuses and in the Current Population Survey are to be highly commended.[14]

Secular changes in labor force participation rates may be expected in the decades ahead. Differential rates of change in the various subgroupings of the population are certain to follow continuing social and economic change in our society and changes in our population size and structure. A better understanding of the secular trend in the size and composition of the labor force may be regarded as a prerequisite to intelligent consideration of other forms of labor mobility.

PROJECTED FUTURE LABOR FORCE

It is not possible to predict with assurance what the future size and composition of the labor force will be. Even though the proportion of people of working age has remained relatively stable during the period for which observation is possible, the size and composition of the labor force is, in some measure, dependent upon the size and composition of future population. Both the growth of population and the growth of the labor force will be influenced by a number of factors

[13] Some research on this problem does point the way to the types of study needed. For example, see Lloyd Reynolds, *op. cit.*, and Charles A. Myers and George T. Shultz, *op. cit.*

[14] The statistical program of the Bureau of the Census has been reduced by reason of a considerable reduction in funds for fiscal year 1954. Labor force statistics are not likely to be expanded in the near future.

which in the present state of knowledge are completely unpredictable, such as swings in the business cycle and war. Estimates of future population, and therefore of the labor force, to the extent that they are dependent on estimates of the future course of the birth rate, are subject to great error as recent experience has demonstrated.[15]

Even if the future population and the labor force cannot be accurately predicted, it is possible to make projections of the size and composition of the population and the labor force on the basis of explicitly stated assumptions. Such projections have indeed been made and are useful for analytical and planning purposes as models of the possible course of events if the assumptions should hold.

The Bureau of the Census has prepared projections of the labor force by sex and age at 5-year intervals from 1950 to 1975. These are summarized in Table 4. These projections are based on projections of the population [16] and in general on an extrapolation of age-sex-specific labor force participation rates from 1920 to the period following World War II—the average from 1947 to 1951.[17] The projections assume a "prosperous peacetime economy"—an economy at a full employment level.

In accordance with these projections the labor force between 1950 and 1975 would increase by some 24 million persons, about 13 million males and 11 million females. Women would become an increasingly important part of the total labor force because they would continue to outnumber men in the total population and because the projection assumes a continuation of their expanding labor force participation. By 1975, women would make up 33% of the labor force as contrasted with 28% in 1950 and 21% in 1920.

[15] J. S. Davis, "The Population Upsurge in the United States," *Food Research Institute, War-Peace Pamphlet 12,* Dec. 1949; also "Our Changed Population Outlook and Its Significance," *Am. Econ. Review,* June 1952, pp. 304–325.

[16] The population projections are described by the Bureau of the Census as "rough revisions and extensions of the medium series of projections of the age-sex distribution of the population published in *Current Population Reports,* Series P-25, No. 43. They are consistent with the revised medium series of projections of total population published in *Current Population Reports,* Series P-25, No. 58, and take into account provisional data on the age and sex distribution of the population from the 1950 Census."

[17] Actually the 1920 Census data adjusted for comparability with the "labor force concept" and the current population survey data for 1947–1951 were used in the analysis of trend. The labor force level as reported in *Current Population Survey* rather than in the 1950 Decennial Census was used as the basis for the projection. For more detailed description of method, see Bureau of the Census, *Current Population Reports, Labor Force,* Series P-50, No. 42, Dec. 10, 1952.

TABLE 4. ESTIMATED TOTAL LABOR FORCE AND LABOR FORCE PARTICIPATION
RATES, BY AGE AND SEX, UNITED STATES, APRIL 1950–1975

	1950 [1]	1955	1960	1965	1970	1975
			Total Labor Force			
Both Sexes, 14 years old and over	64,462,000	67,950,000	72,280,000	78,142,000	83,953,000	88,593,000
Male, 14 years old and over	46,538,000	48,195,000	50,317,000	53,467,000	56,677,000	59,234,000
14 to 19 years	3,177,000	3,383,000	3,943,000	4,825,000	4,589,000	3,758,000
20 to 24 years	5,110,000	4,782,000	5,144,000	6,205,000	7,549,000	7,624,000
25 to 34 years	11,314,000	11,410,000	10,852,000	10,908,000	12,510,000	15,237,000
35 to 44 years	10,312,000	10,838,000	11,336,000	11,414,000	10,820,000	10,892,000
45 to 54 years	8,195,000	8,823,000	9,599,000	10,075,000	10,508,000	10,559,000
55 to 64 years	5,816,000	6,183,000	6,526,000	7,028,000	7,626,000	7,988,000
65 years and over	2,614,000	2,776,000	2,917,000	3,012,000	3,075,000	3,176,000
Female, 14 years old and over	17,924,000	19,755,000	21,963,000	24,675,000	27,276,000	29,359,000
14 to 19 years	1,749,000	1,863,000	2,195,000	2,718,000	2,608,000	2,166,000
20 to 24 years	2,605,000	2,495,000	2,762,000	3,454,000	4,357,000	4,546,000
25 to 34 years	4,039,000	4,305,000	4,258,000	4,414,000	5,242,000	6,634,000
35 to 44 years	4,109,000	4,707,000	5,258,000	5,571,000	5,476,000	5,663,000
45 to 54 years	3,115,000	3,654,000	4,312,000	4,854,000	5,347,000	5,604,000
55 to 64 years	1,725,000	2,055,000	2,384,000	2,759,000	3,231,000	3,607,000
65 years and over	582,000	676,000	794,000	905,000	1,015,000	1,139,000
			Labor Force Participation Rate [2]			
Both Sexes, 14 years old and over	57.0	57.0	56.9	56.7	57.4	58.4
Male, 14 years old and over	83.3	82.4	81.1	79.7	79.7	80.6
14 to 19 years	48.9	47.8	46.7	45.7	44.7	43.7
20 to 24 years	88.6	88.3	88.0	87.6	87.3	86.9
25 to 34 years	96.4	96.4	96.5	96.5	96.5	96.6
35 to 44 years	96.8	96.8	96.9	96.9	96.9	97.0
45 to 54 years	94.3	94.3	94.2	94.2	94.2	94.1
55 to 64 years	87.0	86.9	86.8	86.8	86.7	86.6
65 years and over	44.7	42.9	41.2	39.6	38.0	36.5
Female, 14 years old and over	31.3	32.6	33.8	34.9	36.2	37.5
14 to 19 years	27.4	27.2	27.0	26.8	26.5	26.3
20 to 24 years	44.4	46.3	48.2	50.0	51.8	53.4
25 to 34 years	33.2	35.2	37.2	39.1	40.9	42.7
35 to 44 years	37.7	40.4	43.0	45.4	47.8	50.1
45 to 54 years	35.7	38.1	40.3	42.5	44.7	46.7
55 to 64 years	25.9	27.6	29.2	30.7	32.3	33.8
65 years and over	8.9	9.0	9.2	9.3	9.4	9.5

[1] The figures for 1950 shown in this table, as well as the estimates for future dates, are based on a projection of labor force data for 1920 and for an average of the years 1947 to 1951. The absolute numbers are obtained by applying the projected labor force participation rates to projection of the population (as of July 1 of each year) based on the *1950 Census of Population and Housing.* The estimates for 1950 differ, therefore, from those already published for April 1950, in the "Monthly Report of the Labor Force," which were based on direct measurements from the *Current Population Survey* and on population projections based on the *1940 Census of Population.* The observed labor force participation rates for April 1950 are shown in Table 4.

[2] Per cent of total population in the age group who are in the labor force.

Source: Bureau of the Census, *loc. cit.* (see note 3, Table 1, p. 13).

The proportion of younger persons of both sexes in the labor force would decrease, as would also the proportion of males 65 years and over. All age groups of women above 20 years in the labor force would increase, with the increase being somewhat greater, proportionately, for women 45 years of age and older.

The actual absolute increase in the labor force would be smaller during the present decade than in the decade from 1960 to 1970. During the present decade increments to the labor force will be relatively small because of the decrease in the size of age groups reaching working age as the result of the low birth rate in the 1930's. The greater increases in the labor force in the decade beginning with 1960 will follow from the increased birth rate of the 1940's. The estimated average annual increase in the labor force by 10-year periods from 1920 to 1950 and by 5-year periods from 1950 to 1975 is shown in Table 5.

TABLE 5.   ESTIMATED AVERAGE ANNUAL INCREASE IN THE TOTAL LABOR
FORCE, UNITED STATES, 1920–1975

Period [1]	Number of Persons [2]	Per Cent Increase [3]
1920 to 1930	732,000	1.6
1930 to 1940	609,000	1.2
1940 to 1950	878,000	1.5
1950 to 1955	698,000	1.1
1955 to 1960	866,000	1.2
1960 to 1965	1,172,000	1.6
1965 to 1970	1,162,000	1.4
1970 to 1975	928,000	1.1

[1] Changes for period 1920 to 1940 derived from decennial census data converted for comparability with current estimates; 1940 to 1950 change from *Current Population Survey* data; 1950 to 1975 changes from projections presented in this report.

[2] Net change for period divided by number of years.

[3] Compounded annually.

Source: Bureau of the Census, *op. cit.* (see note 3, Table 1).

Despite the relatively great changes which would occur under this projection in labor force participation rates of specific age and sex classes, the proportion of persons of working age in the labor force would still remain relatively stable during the next 25 years. The total labor force participation, 57.0 for the 1950 period, would, after some slight decrease during the 1960's, rise only to 58.4 by 1975.

CYCLICAL CHANGE

Adequate data do not exist for the analysis of cyclical changes in the total labor force. Decennial Census data are too widely spaced to portray, in measurable form, labor force changes attendant upon swings in the business cycle. Interest in such changes has been great, however, and in the absence of adequate data a polemical literature has arisen on the effects of prosperity and depression on labor force participation.

In accordance with classical and neo-classical theory it is to be expected that the labor force will expand under conditions of prosperity or full employment and contract under conditions of depression.[18] Yet this presupposition is challenged by conflicting views and fragmentary evidence in respect both to the boom and bust phases of the business cycle.

Classical theory is in apparent conflict with the opinion of many economists that "at least a part of the nation's supply curve of labor has a pronounced negative slope, which means that the higher the price paid for labor the less labor will be supplied."[19] The existence of a negative slope in the curve describing the relationship between labor force participation and income level *at any instant in time* has indeed been reasonably well documented.[20] But this relationship cannot be projected to hold *over time*. The effects of the business cycle on the labor force participation rate as evidenced in the literature are at best obscure and the judgments of economists on this point, contradictory.[21]

Particularly insistent has been the additional-worker theory. Curiously enough this theory has been proposed to explain presumed additions to the labor force during both depression and prosperity. Woy-

[18] E.g., Alfred Marshall, *Principles of Economics,* The Macmillan Co., London, 1898.

[19] Richard A. Lester, *Economics of Labor,* The Macmillan Co., New York, 1947, p. 104. See also all of Chapter 5, for discussion and bibliography.

[20] See pp. 15 and 16.

[21] For example, compare H. G. Pearson, *Full Employment,* Yale University Press, New Haven, 1941, or J. M. Keynes, *The General Theory of Employment, Interest and Money,* Harcourt, Brace, New York, 1936, with Long, *op. cit.,* and Woytinsky, "Additional Workers and the Volume of Unemployment in a Depression," *Social Science Research Council, Pamphlet Series I,* 1940; "Additional Workers on the Labor Market in Depressions: A Reply to Mr. Humphrey," *Journal of Political Economy,* 48:735–739, Oct. 1940; *Three Aspects of Labor Dynamics,* Social Science Research Council, Washington, 1942.

tinsky has proffered the additional-worker theory as an explanation of apparent increase in labor force participation during depressions. According to this theory, the loss of employment by the breadwinner results not only in the breadwinner seeking employment but also in other members of the family joining in the search for work, his wife and/or his children. Thus, the loss of one job adds more than one person to the unemployed and increases, also, the total labor force. This theory has not remained unchallenged. Among its antagonists have been D. D. Humphrey and Clarence Long.[22] Opponents of this theory, while admitting that some additional workers may seek employment following the loss of a job by the breadwinner, believe that other workers, under depression conditions, drop out of the labor force because they believe that no employment is to be found. These latter, it has been held, are large enough in numbers to offset, or more than offset, the additional workers.

The data available for testing this theory are far from satisfactory. The enumerative check census taken as part of the Census of Unemployment of 1937 provided data which lent support to the additional-worker theory. By comparing labor force participation rates by age and sex in 1937 with those reported in the preceding Census of 1930, it seemed clear that the labor force rate of females had appreciably increased while those of males, especially in the older age group, had decreased, and that these changes were significantly off the secular trend line of age-sex-specific labor force rates. Long, however, in the fullest treatment of the other side of the case, found results of the Census of Unemployment of 1937 in conflict with six other sets of data—for Germany in 1933, Great Britain in 1921 and 1931, and 4 states in the United States for which some analysis was possible, namely, Michigan, Pennsylvania, Massachusetts, and Rhode Island. In two other instances, Canada and New Zealand, the additional-worker theory seemed to be supported but not conclusively. Long concludes, "It seems not too risky to throw overboard the depression-born theory that the additional worker is of significant statistical magnitude."[23] Despite this conclusion, however, it seems more reasonable to conclude that better data are needed as a basis for concluding anything in the matter.

[22] D. D. Humphrey, "Alleged Additional Workers in the Measurement of Unemployment," *Journal of Political Economy*, XLVIII, June 1940; C. D. Long, "The Concept of Unemployment," *Quarterly Journal of Economics*, LVII, Nov. 1942; *op. cit.*

[23] *Op. cit.*, Chapter 6, p. 22.

Certainly labor force participation rates of younger and older persons and of women have risen well above secular trend lines during recent years of war and full employment. But it is difficult to interpret these data because of the admixture of war, defense, and prosperity conditions. The analysis of a single boom period under conditions of war is hardly adequate for the determination of the pattern of cyclical change.

It would seem that the additional-worker theory, as it may apply to both depression and prosperity, must await further testing as better data become available. Such data are in fact being accumulated in the form of the "Monthly Report on the Labor Force" issued by the Bureau of the Census. The continuation of this monthly series over a prolonged period will, in time, permit both secular trend and cyclical analysis that can provide more definitive answers to the puzzling questions involved than any which exist at the present time. It is to be hoped that the Bureau of the Census in the collection and presentation of these data will be able to continue its gross change as well as net change reports and that the statistics can include the differentiation of primary and secondary workers, and tabulations on a family basis from time to time. An adequate series of such data is certainly to be preferred to continued polemics on this vital and important issue.

WARTIME CHANGES

For the first time in United States experience, data are available on changes in the labor force during a period of mobilization, demobilization, and partial remobilization. Since the "Monthly Report on the Labor Force" was initiated prior to the 1940 Census and has been conducted ever since, it is possible to obtain reliable data on the expansion and contraction of the labor force during World War II and its aftermath, and on the new expansion with the onset of Korean hostilities.

The major conclusion to be reached from this experience is that the labor force in the United States, at least under duress conditions, can be extremely flexible. From 1940 to 1945 the labor force increased by almost 11 million workers. In mid-year 1940, there were about 58 million persons employed or seeking work. By mid-year 1945, there were about 68 million persons in the labor force, including the armed forces. Of the increase of 11 million workers during this 5-year period, some 3 million represent "normal" increase, that is, increase resulting from normal population growth. The additional 8 million represent what may be regarded as "abnormal increment" to the labor force, resulting from the pressures of war.

During this period the armed forces increased from a few hundred thousand to about 12 million persons. The great expansion in the total labor force did little more than maintain the civilian labor force at about the same size, at a figure of approximately 55 million persons. During the same period civilian employment increased by about 7 million jobs, largely represented by the expanding war industries; unemployment decreased from around 8 million in 1940 to approximately a half million under war manpower and other controls at its low point during the war.

Analysis of the deviations in the labor force during this period by age and sex from the "normal" labor force, that is, the labor force which could have been expected if there had been no war, discloses the sources of the added workers from among the "labor reserves." These deviations are shown for two periods, April 1945 and April 1946, in Table 6. April 1945 may be taken as the date approximating full mobilization and maximum labor force participation; April 1946 as approximating the low in the period of demobilization.

It is to be observed that in April 1945 the actual labor force of 66,246,000 persons was over 8 million above the "normal" labor force of 58,163,000. This excess was 13.9% of normal. The total male excess was 9.2% of normal, that of female 26.6%. Almost 4,200,000 females entered the labor force as part of the abnormal increment, as contrasted with only 3,900,000 males.

Analyzed by age, by far the largest single element in the abnormal increment was contributed by young persons 14 to 19 years. Over 2,100,000 young men and 1,450,000 young women, 14 to 19 years old, entered the labor force during these five years in excess over normal. Young males appeared in the labor force in an excess 81.1% above normal; young females in an excess 114.5% above normal.

Older persons, those 65 years of age and over, contributed the next largest proportionate share to the abnormal increment. Almost half a million males, 24.5% in excess over normal, and 161,000 females, 48.9% over normal, swelled the ranks of workers. About 2 million additional workers were gained from females 35 to 65 years of age. Those 35 to 44 represented an excess of 20.1% of normal; those 45 to 54, 37.9% of normal; those 55 to 64, 44.9% of normal. Finally about 1,300,000 additional workers were recruited from males 20 to 64 years of age.

As the net effect of these changes, while the civilian labor force remained approximately the same size, between 54 and 55 million per-

TABLE 6. DEVIATION OF LABOR FORCE FROM "NORMAL," BY AGE AND SEX,
UNITED STATES, 1945 AND 1946

Numbers of Persons in Thousands

	April 1946				April 1945			
	Actual Labor Force *	"Normal" Labor Force	Deviation from "Normal" (− denotes less than "normal")		Actual Labor Force *	"Normal" Labor Force	Deviation from "Normal" (− denotes less than "normal")	
			Number	Per Cent of "Normal"			Number	Per Cent of "Normal"
Both Sexes	60,304	58,843	1450	2.5	66,246	58,163	8083	13.9
Male, total	43,626	42,788	838	2.0	46,407	42,496	3911	9.2
14–19 years	3,431	2,552	879	34.4	4,737	2,615	2122	81.1
20–24 years	4,832	5,386	−554	−10.3	5,829	5,401	428	7.9
25–34 years	10,504	10,948	−444	−4.1	10,575	10,462	113	1.1
35–44 years	9,045	9,070	−25	−0.3	9,453	9,334	119	1.3
45–54 years	8,084	7,863	221	2.8	8,017	7,749	268	3.5
55–64 years	5,349	5,019	330	6.6	5,385	4,998	387	7.7
65 years and over	2,381	1,950	431	22.1	2,411	1,937	474	24.5
Female, total	16,678	16,066	612	3.8	19,839	15,667	4172	26.6
14–19 years	1,930	1,227	703	57.3	2,720	1,268	1452	114.5
20–24 years	2,876	3,037	−161	−5.3	3,405	3,034	371	12.2
25–34 years	3,784	4,508	−724	−16.1	4,551	4,365	186	4.3
35–44 years	3,677	3,543	134	3.8	4,089	3,404	685	20.1
45–54 years	2,651	2,305	346	15.0	2,964	2,149	815	37.9
55–64 years	1,350	1,112	238	21.4	1,620	1,118	502	44.9
65 years and over	410	334	76	22.8	490	329	161	48.9

* Includes Armed Forces.

Source: Derived from U. S. Bureau of the Census data.

sons from April 1940 to April 1945, the number of male civilian workers decreased by over 6 million while the number of female workers increased by over 5½ million.

The remarkable flexibility of the labor force in expanding under war conditions was matched by its ability to contract with demobilization. By April 1946 the labor force had shrunk by almost 6 million persons to total some 60,304,000 workers. Although the working population was, in 1946, 2.5% in excess of normal, the relationship of the actual labor force to the normal labor force varied widely by sex and age. Males were 2.0% in excess of normal, while females were still 3.8% in excess of normal labor force participation. The excess of over 800,000 males was the net effect of a deficit of over 1,000,000 males, mainly 20 to 34 years of age, and an excess of about 1,800,000 males, 14 to 19 years of age, and over 45 years of age. Most of the excess was concentrated among youth under 20 and older workers over 65—the former amounting to almost 900,000 and the latter to over 400,000. The deficit of males 20 to 34 years of age is largely accounted for by the demobilized veterans who under the "G.I. Bill" were continuing their education. The excess of males at the other ages resulted from the maintenance of a relatively large military establishment and the post-war boom which produced full employment.

The excess of approximately 600,000 females in the labor force was the net effect of a deficit of about 900,000 females primarily in the ages 20 to 34 years and an excess in the other age groups, especially in young women 14 to 19 years of age. The relatively large deficit in women of reproductive age is to be accounted for by the dramatic upsurge in both the marriage and birth rates; while the excess in the other age groups also reflected the continuing demand for labor in the post-war boom.

The more recent data reflect the effects of mobilization for the Korean hostilities and continued and heightened prosperity conditions. The average monthly labor force (including the Armed Forces) for the year 1952, 66,400,000, exceeded that for any previous year in United States history, including 1944, the peak year during World War II. The over-all average monthly labor force participation rate in 1952, however, 57%, was below that for 1944 when it reached about 63%. The effects of mobilization, demobilization, and remobilization on age-sex-specific participation rates are shown in Table 7.

On the basis of the rates for year 1940, it is evident that the over-all labor force rate increased by 15% with full mobilization in 1945, and decreased to a level only 5% above the 1940 level with demobilization in 1946. The over-all rate was 1 percentage point above the 1946 level with partial remobilization for the Korean outbreak in 1952.

For all males 14 years of age and over, the increase in labor force participation was 9% with mobilization in 1945, only 1% above the 1940 level with demobilization in 1946, and 2% above the 1940 level with partial remobilization in 1952. Female labor force participation increased 35% between 1940 and 1945, decreased with demobilization in 1946 to a level 12% above the 1940 level, and rose again to a level 18% above the 1940 level by 1952.

The over-all labor force participation rate, and rates by sex for persons 14 years and over, obscure the important age differentials which can be observed. The participation rate of young males 14 to 19

TABLE 7. INDEX OF CHANGES IN LABOR FORCE PARTICIPATION RATES WITH MOBILIZATION, DEMOBILIZATION, AND REMOBILIZATION, APRIL, 1940–1952

	Labor Force Participation Rate				Index of Change (1940 = 100)			
	1940	1945	1946	1952	1940	1945	1946	1952
Both Sexes, 14 years and over	54.1	62.0	56.8	57.2	100	115	105	106
Male, 14 years and over	80.9	87.9	82.0	82.7	100	109	101	102
14–19 years	38.4	67.2	49.6	46.4	100	175	129	121
20–24 years	89.2	96.3	80.1	91.4	100	108	90	102
25–34 years	96.3	97.3	92.4	96.3	100	101	96	100
35–44 years	96.6	97.4	95.8	96.7	100	101	99	100
45–54 years	93.7	95.8	95.0	94.6	100	102	101	101
55–64 years	85.6	90.5	89.0	86.0	100	106	104	100
65 years and over	43.3	49.9	48.3	40.9	100	115	112	94
Female, 14 years and over	27.4	37.0	30.8	32.3	100	135	112	118
14–19 years	19.9	39.6	28.6	27.8	100	199	144	140
20–24 years	47.8	55.6	47.2	43.4	100	116	99	91
25–34 years	35.3	40.5	33.2	34.6	100	115	94	98
35–44 years	29.2	40.6	36.2	39.6	100	139	124	136
45–54 years	24.2	36.7	31.3	39.1	100	152	129	162
55–64 years	17.8	27.1	22.9	27.0	100	152	129	152
65 years and over	6.7	9.4	7.7	8.0	100	140	115	119

Source: Computed from data of Bureau of the Census.

years of age increased by 75% between 1940 and 1945, declined to a level 29% above the 1940 level by 1946, and continued to decline to a level 20% above the 1940 level in 1952. This continuous decline in the labor force participation of youths undoubtedly reflects the decrease in the size of the Armed Forces and the return of increasing numbers of young men to school after the peak of emergency employment during World War II.

Young men 20 to 34 years of age show a strikingly different pattern. Those 20 to 24 years of age show an increase of 8% between 1940 and 1945, and then drop to 10% below the 1940 level with demobilization in 1946. By 1952 they were up to 2% above the 1940 level. The men in this age category did not show so marked a rise in labor force participation as a result of the war and the increase in Armed Forces, since almost 90% of them were already in the labor force in 1940. The relative deficit in labor force participation, with demobilization, is attributable to the continuation of schooling, as indicated above, under "the G.I. Bill." With partial mobilization in 1952 and the expiration of most of the schooling benefits of the G.I.'s by this date, the labor force participation rate rose slightly above the 1940 level. The pattern for males 25 to 34 years of age is of similar character but with smaller increases and decreases with the changing course of events.

Males 35 to 54 years of age showed practically no change in labor force participation rates throughout this period, although slight increase is evident for males 45 to 54 under conditions of war and full employment. Men 55 to 64 years of age increased in labor force participation by 6% between 1940 and 1945, declined by only 2 percentage points with demobilization, and were back at the 1940 level even under conditions of partial mobilization in 1952. Older males, those 65 years and older, showed an increase of 15% in labor force participation by 1945, declined only 3 percentage points under conditions of full employment with demobilization in 1946, but dropped 6% below the 1946 level by 1952. The decrease in the labor force participation of older men is undoubtedly attributable to a return to the secular trend downward in labor force participation of men in this age class, accelerated by the amendment of the Social Security Act of 1951 which broadened coverage and liberalized benefits.

Female labor force participation rates increased more than male with mobilization, remaining at a relatively high level with demobilization, and rose more than male with partial mobilization. Young women under 20 almost doubled their labor force participation rates between 1940 and 1945, were still 44% above the 1940 level in 1946, and declined by only 4 percentage points to a level 40% above the 1940 level by 1952. Women 20 to 34 years of age, the period of greatest reproductivity, increased their labor force participation rate by only 15% with mobilization and were below their 1940 labor force participation rates, both with demobilization after the war and during the period of partial remobilization in 1952. Relatively low labor force participation rates of this class of women was the direct result of the very high post-war marriage and birth rates.

Among women 35 years of age and older the effects of high-level economic activity after the war and partial mobilization with the Korean outbreak are most evident. Women in these age classes with maturing or no children had relatively high labor force participation rates under mobilization conditions in 1945, ranging from 39 to 52% above 1940 levels. With demobilization in 1946 women 35 to 64 years of age were still in the labor force at levels 24 to 29% above the 1940 level; and under conditions of partial mobilization, their labor force activity rose considerably, resulting in 1952 levels ranging from 36 to 62% above the 1940 levels. Even among women 65 years of age and over, in contrast with older men, there was some increase in labor force participation between 1946 and 1952.

An analysis of labor force participation rates in 1952 as deviations from the normal labor force is not undertaken, because of the many problems which arise in attempting to project normal rates into the post-war years. Construction of generally acceptable normal participation rates throughout this period must await the accumulation of longer series of data which will permit the analysis of secular trend apart from the disturbing influences of cyclical and war changes.[24]

The United States was in a particularly good position in respect to its labor potential at the onset of the war. After the relatively low marriage and birth rates of the depression 30's, women were relatively free for employment under the pressures of war. Moreover, the increasing rate of retirement of older workers and relatively high school attendance of youth in this country provided additional reservoirs of labor which could be tapped in the emergency. Should mobilization again be necessary, in the near future, the situation for adding to the labor force would not be nearly so favorable. Our high marriage and birth rates have decreased the potentialities of employment for women, and the continuing high labor force participation of the young and old has decreased these potential reserves for labor force additions. Under such circumstances a new war effort would require much more in the way of reallocation of persons already in the labor force than was the case during World War II.

The availability of monthly statistics on the labor force during the war, permitting an analysis of the type presented above, has greatly enriched our knowledge of ingress to and egress from the labor force under war conditions. The accumulation of similar data over a prolonged period of time would undoubtedly illuminate the many ques-

[24] Reynolds and Long are among those who disagree with the census definition of "normal" for the wartime analysis. See Lloyd Reynolds, "Economics of Labor," *A Survey of Contemporary Economics*, Blakiston, Philadelphia, 1948, p. 271; and Clarence Long, *The Labor Force in Wartime America*, p. 64ff.

Long has made similar analysis of wartime changes for England, Canada, and Germany. Each of these countries was able to expand its total labor force during the war, although none of them, as Long points out, were able to do so to the extent necessary to maintain a total normal civilian labor force. See *op. cit.*, Chapter 7, also in *The Labor Force in Wartime America*, p. 65. In the United States, as has been indicated, the total civilian labor force remained at about the same size from 1940 to 1945. But this did not allow for normal growth.

tions which are still unresolved in respect to labor force participation in the long run and in the course of business cycle swings.

SEASONAL CHANGES

Many of our economic activities are affected by the changing seasons. Seasonal variations in employment, especially in agriculture and industry for which data have been available, have been known for some time. But seasonal variations in the total labor force, as well as in its components—the employed and unemployed—have been known only since the initiation of the Monthly Report on the Labor Force. Even now, however, as the result of the abnormal conditions which have prevailed throughout most of the life of this statistical series, only approximate seasonal indexes can be constructed.

A summary of seasonal variations in the size of the labor force has been constructed by Durand for the period 1940 to 1944.[25] He reports "average deviations of monthly figures from annual averages" during this period as follows:

January	−1,800,000	July	+2,500,000
February	−1,700,000	August	+2,200,000
March	−1,600,000	September	+500,000
April	−800,000	October	−300,000
May	....	November	−600,000
June	+1,700,000	December	−1,000,000

These data indicate the seasonal swing in size of the labor force of about 4,300,000 persons, or about 8% from a trough in January to a peak in July. The most important single seasonal factor seems to be school attendance which is responsible for the great increase in the labor force in June and July and the drop in August and September. Seasonal agricultural changes contribute to the effects of the school cycle and are a major element in the lows of January through March. As might be expected, the elements of the labor force that showed the largest seasonal variations are young persons under 25 and women, especially in agriculture.

The relatively large swing in the labor force by season points to the importance of seasonal corrections in the data when temporal comparisons are made. Such corrections are possible only in a crude fashion in the present state of the data and are not yet published by the

[25] *Op. cit.*, p. 138. These figures are for data as originally published by the Bureau of the Census. Revised figures comparable with current data by Durand, in an unpublished manuscript, are reproduced in Jaffe and Stewart, *op. cit.*, p. 155.

Bureau of the Census, although it has been working on the problem. It is necessary in making temporal comparisons in labor force data, therefore, to control seasonality by using either annual averages or the same month each year, for year to year comparisons.

OTHER SHORT-RUN CHANGES

Analysis of changes in the labor force other than those attributable to secular trend, cyclical fluctuation, and seasonality is difficult in the absence of data permitting better measurement of the labor force over a prolonged period of time. From the data that are available, it is clear that the net change in the total labor force or proportion of persons of working age who are workers must necessarily be small in the short run.

Long, particularly, emphasizes the small magnitude of short-run changes in the over-all participation rate when it is adjusted for seasonal changes. Under conditions of relatively high unemployment, between April 1940 and December 1941, "maximum deviation of the labor force was 2 million below its high employment normal, amounting to 3.5 per cent of the over-all labor force and about 2 per cent of the working age population." Under high employment conditions, from mid-1946 to mid-1949, he found that the "labor force remained within 1½ per cent of normal" and that "related to the working-age population, the maximum plus or minus deviation was 1 per cent." [26]

On the basis of his studies of the relation between income and labor force participation, Long concludes that the "labor force as the proportion of the working age population is completely inelastic with respect to short-run changes in real or money incomes per worker." This finding is inconsistent with classical or neo-classical labor theory [27] and points up the need for renewed activity both in theory and research, dealing with the explanation of short-run changes on the size and composition of the labor force. Durand's observation, made in 1948, is still apposite: "Analysis of the effects of economic factors upon labor

[26] *Op. cit.*, Chapter 8, p. 2. Despite the relatively small changes in over-all labor force participation on the short run, Long did find an association between changes in the worker participation rate and fluctuations in unemployment and the size of the armed forces. Labor force participation drops with a decrease in employment and rises with military expansion.

[27] For a summary of early theory, see Paul Douglas, *The Theory of Wages*, The Macmillan Co., New York, 1934. See also Richard A. Scoter, *Economics of Labor*, The Macmillan Co., New York, 1947, Chapter V; and John Durand, *op. cit.*, p. 84ff.

force trends over either short or long periods is made most difficult by lack of adequate data." [28]

It should perhaps be mentioned again, at this point, that reasonably good documentation exists on the inverse relationship at a given time between income level and extent of labor force participation of workers—especially women and younger and older workers. Long's studies, as has been indicated, confirm Schoenberg and Douglas's earlier studies on the correlation between the level of labor force participation and income level for various cities and urban areas at selected dates.[29] Moreover, the 1940 census tabulations demonstrate the inverse correlation between wage and salary income of husbands and the labor force participation rate of women.[30] These data restricted to cross-section analysis *at a given instant in time,* however, can in no wise be interpreted as indicating any correlation between labor force participation and income level *over time.*

Gross Changes. The relatively small changes in over-all labor force participation rates obscure the fact that there is indeed great mobility in labor force participation even from month to month. The number of shifts into and out of the labor force, that is, the shuttling back and forth between the categories "in the labor force" and "not in the labor force" are of considerable magnitude. The Bureau of the Census since 1945 has been publishing data on "gross changes" in the labor force which disclose a surprisingly large number of persons who change their status as in, or not in, the labor force each month despite the relative stability of the total number of workers and the proportion of persons of working age who are workers. These data for 1951 are summarized in Table 8 by sex and age.

For the labor force as a whole in 1951, the average number of persons who changed their status in respect to labor force participation from one month to the next constituted over 10% of the average monthly number of persons in the labor force. Male "entrances" and "exits," [31] however, were less than 6% of the total average monthly male labor force; female entrances and exits made up 22% of the average monthly female labor force. These data provide a more adequate basis for the

[28] *Op. cit.,* p. 85.

[29] *Op. cit.,* Chapter 3.

[30] E.g., see Jaffe and Stewart, *op. cit.,* p. 140.

[31] "Entrances" and "exits" are used to refer to a change in status from one month to the next in respect to labor force participation. If a given person changed status more than once during the month, only one change would be counted. Similarly if a person changed status but reverted to the same status he had in the preceding month no change would be counted.

TABLE 8. GROSS CHANGES IN THE CIVILIAN LABOR FORCE BY SEX AND AGE,
UNITED STATES, 1951

Gross Change	Total (in thousands)	Age				
		14–19 yr	20–24 yr	25–44 yr	45–64 yr	65 yr and over
Total						
Average number in labor force	62,871	4984	6668	28,712	19,486	3024
Average monthly gross change	6,627	1797	816	1,939	1,516	560
Number additions	3,320	952	383	968	758	259
Number reductions	3,307	845	433	971	758	301
Average gross change as percentage of average labor force	10.5	36.1	12.2	6.8	7.8	18.5
Male						
Average number in labor force	43,647	2967	3999	20,156	14,062	2465
Average monthly gross change	2,419	1009	273	352	431	356
Number additions	1,192	537	114	163	209	170
Number reductions	1,227	472	159	189	222	186
Average gross change as percentage of average labor force	5.5	34.0	6.8	1.7	3.1	14.4
Female						
Average number in labor force	19,224	2018	2670	8,556	5,424	558
Average monthly gross change	4,208	789	543	1,586	1,086	205
Number additions	2,128	416	269	804	550	89
Number reductions	2,080	373	274	782	536	116
Average gross change as percentage of average labor force	21.9	39.1	20.3	18.5	20.0	36.7

Note: Data are rounded independently in thousands and may not add to totals.

Source: Compiled from Bureau of the Census, "Annual Report on the Labor Force for 1950 and 1951," *Current Population Reports*, Series P-50, Nos. 31 and 40, March 1951 and May 1952, Tables 3, 16, and 17.

conclusion that male mobility in respect to labor force participation is much smaller than female, as is evident in the analysis of gross changes by age. This is particularly true of males 25 to 64 years of age. Male workers 25 to 64 years of age seem to constitute the hard core of the labor force in that there is not only negligible net change in this group in the course of any given year but, also, very small gross change. Total entrances and exits combined for men 25 to 64 years of age during 1951 constituted only 2 to 3% of total males in the labor force.

By far the greatest mobility in labor force participation occurs among younger persons under 20 years of age. Entrances and exits of males in this age group in 1951 were in number about ⅓ of the total number of young men in the labor force. For females in the same age category these gross changes made up about ⅖ of their total average number for the year.

Gross changes among males dropped sharply from those under 20, to those 20 to 24 years of age, when in 1951 they made up about 7% of the total. This percentage drops even more sharply among those 25 to 44 years when they make up less than 2%; and rises somewhat among males 45 to 64 years when they make up 3% of the total. The increase of males in the last age group is undoubtedly greater in the older workers in this group for whom separate data are not available. This is strongly suggested by the fact that, among males 65 years old and over, entrances and exits increased to over 14% of the total.

Among females there is also a great drop in the proportion of gross changes from the age group 14 to 19 years to the age group 20 to 24 years. The drop, however, is not nearly so great as for males, and the proportionate level of gross changes among young women 20 to 24 years is about 3 times as high as that for males. The greatest contrast in labor force participation between males and females in our society, however, is indicated by the gross changes for the age groups 25 to 64 years. Whereas for males gross changes are practically negligible, for females of this age, entrances and exits constitute about a fifth of the total in the labor force, a proportion 6 to 9 times as great as that for males. Among older women, those 65 years old and over, gross changes increased to a level of over $\frac{1}{3}$ of the total in the labor force.

The gross change analysis contained in the above paragraphs does not, of course, refer to individuals—that is, the total number of "entrances" and "exits," as defined, is much greater than the total number of persons who actually entered or left the labor force. It is undoubtedly true as is known for other forms of labor mobility [32] that a relatively small proportion of the total workers contributed a disproportionately large share of the mobility. This is at least suggested by relating the total number of monthly gross changes during the year to the monthly average number of persons in the labor force. The total number of monthly additions to the labor force was almost 40 million or almost $\frac{2}{3}$ of the monthly average of 62,781,000 workers. The total number of monthly reductions was approximately of the same magnitude. Entrances and exits, combined, aggregated almost 80 million. Obviously double counting of shifts and persons is involved, since many of the mobile persons both entered and left the labor force during the year; and many persons undoubtedly entered and left the labor force more than once during the course of the year. The total number of entrances and exits for males approximated 29 million in relation to an average annual labor force of 43,647,000; for females the aggregate number of entrances and exits was about 50 million in relation to an

[32] E.g., see forthcoming volume, Gladys L. Palmer, *Labor Mobility in Six Cities*, Social Science Research Council, New York.

average annual labor force of 19,224,000. Gross changes of this magnitude led the National Association of Manufacturers to state: "Actually the apparent stability of the labor force and employment concepts is an illusion." [33] They call attention to the fact that between January and February 1950 when the total civilian labor force increased by 210,000, some 7,436,000 persons made some shift in labor force status during that month, including shifts among the various categories of labor force status and persons not in the labor force. In respect to labor force participation alone, the 210,000-person increase was the net result of 2,445,000 persons entering the labor force and 2,236,000 persons leaving the labor force.

The implication of such great mobility in labor force participation, especially for women and for younger and older persons, has not yet been clearly grasped by the economist, the sociologist, the business man, or the policy maker. It is probably erroneous to conclude, as does the National Association of Manufacturers from its analysis of gross changes in respect to unemployment, "that unemployment as measured by the Bureau of the Census does not have a very clear cut significance. Large numbers of individuals drift in and out of 'the unemployed,' apparently on a somewhat casual basis and for reasons which may have little to do with the labor market. . . . The chart accompanying this memo shows how complicated the situation really is, and how easily the net result in any particular month can be fortuitous rather than significant." [34]

This quick conclusion that the large magnitude of gross changes indicates that much labor force participation is "casual" or not "significant" is hardly warranted in a free economy. On the other hand, the N.A.M. is undoubtedly on solid ground in indicating that it drew attention to the data on gross changes in the labor force "to correct the erroneous impression arising from the almost exclusive use of the net over-all figures." [35]

The statistics on gross changes in the labor force have perhaps more than any other single type of data emanating from the Monthly Report on the Labor Force illuminated the complex character of labor force dynamics. Moreover, they strongly indicate the need for similar data on gross change as well as net change for the analysis of all temporal changes in the size and composition of the working force.

[33] "The Meaning of Unemployment Statistics as Revealed by Gross Changes in the Labor Force," *Economic Policy Division Series, No. 29,* August 1950, p. 3.
[34] *Ibid.,* p. 9.
[35] *Ibid.,* p. 9.

WORKING LIFE

The application of the life table technique to labor force activity has further illuminated various aspects of labor force participation.[36] It has provided not only an important tool for measuring the average length of working life but also for showing the pattern of entrance to and exit from labor force activity. Unfortunately, the technique has as yet been employed only for the analysis of male labor force participation, because of the greater technical difficulties involved in applying it to female workers.

An abridged table of working life for males for 1940 and 1947 is shown in Table 9. More detailed data by individual years of age have also been published by the Bureau of Labor Statistics.[37] The abridged life table permits a number of interesting observations.

To begin with, at age 15 to 19, males, in 1940, could expect to live, on the average, an additional 51.3 years and to be members of the labor force for an additional 45.8 years. They could therefore anticipate an average period of 5.5 years of life after exit from the labor force. By 1947, expectation of life for this group had increased by 1.3 years, but expectation of labor force participation had increased by 1.6 years. Thus, despite the decrease in mortality, the post-war conditions of labor force participation, as contrasted with those in 1940, resulted in a decrease of 0.3 year in the number of years of life remaining after exit from the labor force. This, of course, is a summary way of indicating that in 1947 a larger proportion of males, especially older males, were in the labor force under post-war conditions than had been the case in 1940.

The greater labor force potential in the male population in 1947 than that of 1940 may also be readily quantified and summarized. The sum of the entries in column 3 represents the "stationary labor force," paralleling the sum of the entries in column 2 which represents "the stationary population." These aggregates may be interpreted as indicating, respectively, the total number of man years in the labor force, and of life, which would be experienced by a cohort of 100,000 males under the mortality and labor force conditions of the given year to which they refer. Thus in 1940, the total man years in the labor force which would be experienced by a cohort of 100,000 men under the

---

[36] W. S. Woytinsky, *Labor in the United States,* Social Science Research Council, 1938, pp. 261–263. John D. Durand, *op. cit.,* p. 56. "Tables of Working Life," *Bulletin 1001,* Bureau of Labor Statistics, Washington, 1950.

[37] *Ibid.,* p. 4ff.

TABLE 9. ABRIDGED TABLE OF WORKING LIFE, MALES, 1940[1] AND 1947

(1)	(2)	(3)	(4)	(5)	(6)	(7)	(8)	(9)	(10)
	Number Living of 100,000 Born Alive			Accessions to the Labor Force (per 1000 in population)	Separations from the Labor Force (per 1000 in labor force)			Average Number of Remaining Years of	
Age Interval	In Population	In Labor Force			Due to All Causes	Due to Death	Due to Retirement	Life	Labor Force Participation
		Number	Per Cent of Population						
x to $x+n$	$_nL_x$	$_nLw_x$	$_nw_x$	$1000\ _nA_x$	$1000\ _nQ_x^s$	$1000\ _nQ_x^d$	$1000\ _nQ_x^r$	$\overset{\circ}{e}_x$	$\overset{\circ}{e}w_x$
	Within Age Interval			Between Successive Age Intervals				At Beginning of Age Interval	
1940									
10–14	461,865	6,196	2	431.0	8.2	8.2	.....	....	....
15–19	458,100	205,229	44.8	441.6	12.0	12.0	.....	51.3	45.8
20–24	452,589	405,067	89.5	68.0	14.9	14.9	.....	46.8	41.3
25–29	445,845	429,795	96.4	7.9	17.6	17.6	.....	42.4	36.8
30–34	438,014	425,750	97.2	.....	28.0	21.9	6.1	38.0	32.3
35–39	428,373	413,808	96.6	.....	37.8	29.7	8.1	33.7	28.0
40–44	415,611	398,155	95.8	.....	53.3	42.1	11.2	29.6	23.8
45–49	398,028	376,933	94.7	.....	80.2	60.8	19.4	25.5	19.8
50–54	373,582	346,684	92.8	.....	117.8	85.9	31.9	21.8	16.0
55–59	340,970	305,850	89.7	.....	211.6	115.7	95.9	18.3	12.4
60–64	299,545	241,134	80.5	.....	376.7	148.9	227.8	15.1	9.2
65–69	248,456	150,316	60.5	.....	495.5	191.8	303.7	12.2	6.8
70–74	189,583	75,833	40.0	.....	576.4	262.4	314.0	9.6	5.6
75 and over	232,278	44,830	19.3	.....	.....	.....	.....	....	....
1947									
10–14	475,284	18,320	2	524.1	5.8	5.8	.....	....	....
15–19	472,525	259,889	55.0	346.7	9.5	9.5	.....	52.6	47.4
20–24	468,041	421,237	90.0	67.2	11.3	11.3	.....	48.0	42.8
25–29	462,739	447,931	96.8	6.9	12.6	12.6	.....	43.5	38.2
30–34	456,917	445,494	97.5	.....	20.7	16.6	4.1	39.0	33.6
35–39	449,323	436,293	97.1	.....	32.5	24.4	8.1	34.5	29.1
40–44	438,330	422,112	96.3	.....	47.9	36.7	11.2	30.2	24.8
45–49	422,149	401,886	95.2	.....	75.6	56.3	19.3	26.0	20.7
50–54	398,186	371,508	93.3	.....	106.7	82.1	24.6	22.1	16.9
55–59	365,102	331,878	90.9	.....	160.5	115.1	45.4	18.6	13.2
60–64	322,102	278,618	86.5	.....	354.7	148.6	206.1	15.3	9.7
65–69	267,931	179,782	67.1	.....	501.8	189.2	312.6	12.4	7.0
70–74	204,978	89,575	43.7	.....	544.3	258.8	285.5	9.9	5.9
75 and over	263,826	60,944	23.1	.....	.....	.....	.....	....	....

[1] Labor force data for 1940 have been adjusted to allow for a revision in Census Bureau enumeration procedures introduced in July 1945. The resulting rates are comparable with those shown in the abridged table for 1947, but may not be compared directly with the detailed tables for 1940.

[2] In accordance with current Census definitions, only persons 14 years of age or over are enumerated in the labor force. No meaningful percentage of the population in the labor force could therefore be computed for the age interval 10–14 years.

Source: U. S. Bureau of Labor Statistics.

conditions indicated, would be 3,825,580; under 1947 conditions a total of 4,163,013 man years in the labor force could be expected. In other words, under the mortality and working conditions of 1947 as contrasted with 1940, there would be a 9% increase in labor force potential.

Also significant are the patterns of accessions to and separations from the labor force. In 1940, for example (see column 5), 431 males per 1000, 10 to 14 years of age, entered the labor force in the following 5-year interval. Similarly, the 5-year entry rate of males 15 to 19 years of age for 1940 was 442 per 1000. By 1947, the age of entry had decreased as is indicated by the 5-year entry rate of 524 per 1000 for males 10 to 14 years of age and the drop in entry rate to 347 per 1000 for those 15 to 19 years old. As is to be expected from the relatively high labor force participation rates of males in adult life, practically all accessions to the labor force occur by age 25.

The effects of full employment conditions in 1947, as contrasted with 1940, on separations from the labor force may also be quickly quantified and summarized. In both periods, of course, the total separation rate as well as the separation rates due to deaths and to retirement, respectively (see columns 6, 7, 8), increased with age. Under 1947 conditions, however, there was a noticeable decline in the rate of separation at all ages up to 65 with the greatest drop occurring for males 55 to 59 years old. Some of this reduction in separation rates was attributable to the decrease in the rate of retirement of older men under conditions of war and higher economic activity.

The Bureau of Labor Statistics has also calculated life table functions for white males in 1900 and 1940, and for total males for 1940, 1947, and 1975. Two estimates are presented for 1975 on the average number of years of life remaining for total life, in the labor force and in retirement. Estimates A are based on the assumption of continuing decline in labor force participation rates for men 55 years and older in accordance with the trend from 1920–1940. Estimates B assume labor force participation rates at 1947 high employment levels. The data showing average number of years of life remaining in various categories at age 20 are summarized in Table 10.

Between 1900 and 1940 the expectation of life of white males at age 20 increased by 5.5 years from 42.2 to 47.7 years. During the same four decades, the number of years of life remaining in the labor force at age 20 increased by 2.6 years to a total of 42 years. In consequence the average number of years of life remaining after retirement from the labor force increased from 2.8 to 5.7 years. These data not only effectively summarize changes in labor force participation in relation to

TABLE 10. AVERAGE NUMBER OF REMAINING YEARS OF LIFE, IN LABOR FORCE AND IN RETIREMENT, AT AGE 20; WHITE MALES, 1900, 1940; TOTAL MALES, 1940, 1947, 1975

Year	Total $\overset{\circ}{e}_x$	In Labor Force [1] $\overset{\circ}{e}w_x$	In Retirement $\overset{\circ}{e}_x - \overset{\circ}{e}w_x$
White Males			
1900 [2]	42.2	39.4	2.8
1940	47.7	42.0	5.7
Total Males			
1940	46.8	41.3	5.5
1947	48.0	42.8	5.2
1975 (A) [3]	52.7	42.8	9.9
1975 (B) [3]	52.7	45.9	6.8

[1] Labor force estimates for 1900 and 1940 have been adjusted for comparability with the estimates for 1947 and 1975, but may not be compared directly with the detailed tables for 1940.

[2] Mortality data based on records of 11 original death registration states.

[3] *A:* Assumes continued decline in labor force participation rates for men, 55 years and over, based on 1920–1940 trends. *B:* Assumes labor force participation rates at 1947 levels.

Source: U. S. Dept. of Labor, *loc. cit.* (see Table 8).

the life span, but, also, provide a quantification of the problem of the older person who is faced with the necessity of economic and other forms of adjustment after retirement.

If previous trends are projected, expectation of life at age 20 for all males will increase by 5.9 years to 52.7 years by 1975. If the trends between 1920 and 1940 should continue the average number of years of life remaining in the labor force for total males would increase by 1.5 years between 1940 and 1975 to a total of 42.8 years. This would result in almost a doubling of average number of years of life remaining in retirement from 5.5 years in 1940 to 9.9 years in 1975. If, however, labor force participation rates remain at 1947 post-war levels, the average number of years of life remaining in the labor force would increase by 4.6 years between 1940 and 1975 to a total of 45.9 years. Under these circumstances average number of years of life remaining after retirement would be 6.8 or only 1.3 years greater than that for 1940.

Similar analysis is not available for women. Participation in the labor force, however, follows a quite different pattern for females from that for males. Female age-specific worker rates from 1890 through 1940, although at increasing levels for all but the younger and older age groups, increased from the time of entrance into the labor force to a peak at ages 20 to 24 and then declined continuously to the end of the life span. Under the full-employment and high marriage and fertility conditions of 1950, however, the pattern of labor force participation was significantly different. The female worker rate declined from age group 20 to 24 to the age group 25 to 34 but then rose at

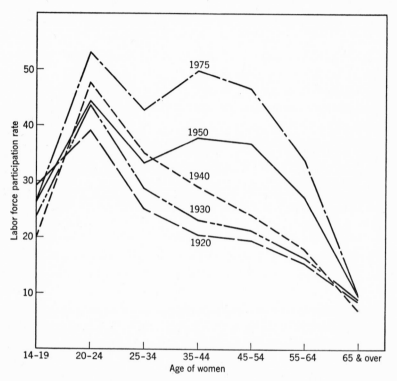

CHART 1.   Female labor force participation rates, United States, 1920–1950 and 1975.

ages 35 to 44, remained relatively high at ages 45 to 54, and then declined sharply thereafter although they were still well above the levels of 1940 and preceding decennial dates (see Chart 1). Thus the war undoubtedly accelerated the previous trend of increasing labor force participation for women in general, and particularly for married women, so as to make quite pronounced the tendency for women to re-enter the labor force after their period of greatest child-bearing and household responsibilities.[38]

[38] The extent of this tendency is indicated in 1951 labor force participation rates for six United States cities where only 11% of the married women 25 to 34 years

In the projections of the future labor force, the greatest relative increases in the participation rates for women occur among women 35 to 54 years of age. Women in this age class would, in 1975, have a labor force rate of about 50% as contrasted with a rate of about 38% for 1950 and a rate of about 20% in 1920. With the small increase in the worker rate projected for younger women aged 20 to 34 years, primarily because of the assumed continuation of high marriage and birth rates under prosperity, the labor force participation rates for women in 1975 would have a more marked upturn at ages 35 to 44 than that which obtained in 1950.

There seems to be an increasing tendency, therefore, for women to enter the labor force before marriage; to drop out during the period of greatest reproductivity and child care during their late twenties and early thirties; to return to the labor force as their children mature; and to drop out again with aging in later years, particularly after age 54. In addition to the relatively high mobility of women in labor force participation which may be more or less continuous as revealed by the gross monthly changes in the labor force, there seems also to be a definite pattern of double entry into the labor force. Although a hard core of women tend to enter and remain in the labor force, increasing numbers tend to enter the first time before marriage and child-bearing, and a second time after their children grow older and household responsibilities decrease.

SUMMARY

The increasing complexity of our society and the growing tendency for specialization in function have resulted in a sharp differentiation of work from other life activities. In consequence, the population may be subdivided into workers and nonworkers—or, to use the current terminology, into persons in the labor force and persons not in the labor force. The categorization of the population into workers and nonworkers, although in the main a relatively simple task, involves many problems for marginal persons, particularly for women, and for younger and older workers in the process of entering or leaving the labor force. The actual number and composition of the labor force is then, in part, a function of the conceptual framework and the methods and measurement used in Census or current survey practices.

old who had children under 6 years old were working, whereas 32% of those with no children under 6 but with children 6 to 17 years old were working. Adapted from Gladys L. Palmer, *op. cit.*

In the United States the measurement of the labor force was obtained in 1930 and in prior Census years through the gainful-worker approach. In the 1940 Census the basic method was changed to the labor-force approach. At about the same time there was also initiated a monthly survey, "The Monthly Report on the Labor Force," which measured the size and composition of the labor force, including employment and unemployment status, on a continuing basis. Analysis of changes in the labor force in the United States is then primarily dependent on the Decennial Census data, beginning with the 1870 Census, and on the monthly data described.

Our changing economy together with its wide cyclical fluctuations and the changing role of the worker, particularly as dramatized in changing labor-management relations since the advent of the "New Deal," has increasingly focused attention on problems relating to the supply and mobility of labor. There has been a renewed and growing interest, public and academic, in the nature of the labor market, and an enhanced interest in empirical research into the labor market and related activities.[39]

As part of this acceleration of research into the labor market and related activities, there has been a growing interest in problems of labor mobility. A summary of a number of aspects of labor mobility research is being published under the aegis of the Social Science Research Council's Labor Market Research Committee, as is also the Committee's relatively large-scale research into labor mobility in six cities.[40] Most research into labor mobility, however, has focused on various types of changes which occur among persons already in the labor force, and only, incidentally, on the whole, on mobility in respect to labor force participation itself. Since all other labor force changes, such as changes in job, employer, occupation, industry, or geographic location,

[39] This growing interest is manifested, among other things, by the creation in 1943, by the Social Science Research Council, of its Labor Market Research Committee, which is still in existence and which has helped to stimulate, as well as has participated in, various forms of labor market research. Other manifestations may be seen in the mushrooming of industrial relations centers in our universities and in the organization of the Industrial Relations Research Association in 1947. Though labor-management relations, especially as evidenced in collective bargaining, is undoubtedly the focal interest of industrial relations centers and of the Industrial Relations Research Association, there is also evident an increasing research interest, among these groups, in the labor market. For a listing of research activities in this field see the Social Science Research Council's *Memorandum on University Research Programs in the Field of Labor, 1950,* New York, 1950.

[40] Herbert Parnes, *op. cit.* Gladys Palmer, *op. cit.*

occur within the framework of the changes of the total labor force, it would seem highly desirable to devote increasing attention to mobility in labor force participation itself, and to place other forms of labor mobility in the context of mobility in labor force participation.[41]

The type of study which is desirable has been roughly outlined in the paradigm which has been outlined above. In brief, it would be highly desirable to study changes in labor force participation, both gross and net, in accordance with standard time series analysis, that is, in its secular, cyclical, seasonal, and other manifestations; in terms of the size and composition of the labor force; in terms of family as well as individual units; and in its space dimensions—that is, national, regional, metropolitan area, and individual labor market areas, etc. Moreover, there is a great need for research in the various types of factors, demographic, economic, cultural, political, and social-psychological associated with labor force changes.

Unfortunately, data are not available for adequate analysis of the type desired. Although the census data in the United States permit some analysis of secular changes on a net basis, the Monthly Labor Force series is available for too short a period of time, as yet, to provide an understanding of cyclical changes, to provide stable seasonal indexes, or to illuminate, as far as is desired, the various forms of residual changes in labor force size and composition. The monthly series, however, has permitted an unprecedented type of analysis of changes in the size and composition of the labor force during a period of mobilization, demobilization, and partial remobilization. It has also made available new information on gross, in addition to net, changes on a monthly basis which reveal a surprisingly high mobility of marginal categories of workers. In these respects the monthly series illustrates the great extension of knowledge which may be expected in respect to other aspects of labor force mobility as the data accumulate.

There is even a greater deficiency in the availability of data and research on the factors associated with these various types of mobility and labor force participation. Certain factors associated with labor force changes are reasonably well documented, particularly the demographic factors which can be readily quantified and for which statistics are available, but the literature in respect to other factors, economic, cultural, political, and "personal" are at best in a rudimentary or speculative stage. Tied in with the analysis of the various factors associated with labor force change is the need for better data on labor force size

[41] Unfortunately, because of limited resources, this was not done in the Committee's own study of mobility in the six cities.

and composition on a family unit basis. Without question, many of the forces which affect labor force participation operate through their effect on the family as a unit, as well as on individual members thereof.[42]

There has been increasing attention in recent years to the labor force and to labor market behavior. Although empirical research is illuminating various types of labor force problems, there still remain large areas of ignorance where polemical debate serves as a poor substitute for evidence. The data indicate that, at least in the short run, the labor force in the aggregate may be relatively inelastic, though its composition is subject to great changes. Research has pointed more and more to the factors other than wages or family income that influence labor force participation. Much remains to be learned, however, on the "why's" of labor mobility, including mobility in labor force participation. It is perhaps in the study of the elements other than wages in the "whole of the advantages and disadvantages of the different employments of labor" that the greatest progress may be made in augmenting our understanding of labor mobility.

Better data are needed on labor force mobility and especially on the various factors associated with changes in labor force participation. Such research may be expected to result in the refinement of existing theory, the development of more comprehensive and apposite theory, and the enrichment of our knowledge of the labor force and the operations of the labor market.

[42] Studies of this type are relatively scarce. A few indicating the complex character of the problem are: Robert C. Angell, *The Family Encounters the Depression,* Scribner, New York, 1936; Ruth Shonle Cavin and Katherine H. Ranck, *The Family and the Depression,* University of Chicago Press, Chicago, 1938; Sanford Dornbusch, *op. cit.;* Paul H. Douglas, *Wages and the Family,* University of Chicago Press, Chicago, 1925; Don H. Humphrey, *Family Unemployment,* W.P.A., Washington, 1940; Hazel Kyrk, *Economic Problems of the Family,* Harper, New York, 1933; Samuel A. Stouffer and Paul F. Lazarsfeld, *Research Memorandum on the Family in the Depression,* Social Science Research Council, New York, 1937. See also 16th Census of the United States, 1940, *Population, Families, Employment Status,* Bureau of the Census, Washington, 1943, and other Census statistics relating to the labor force on a family basis.

3. Interpreting Patterns of Labor Mobility

GLADYS L. PALMER

Research Professor and
Director of the Industrial
Research Unit
Wharton School of
Finance and Commerce
University of Pennsylvania

Other essays in this volume emphasize the patterns of mobility of the average worker in a community, the economic and noneconomic motivations that affect job choice, and some of the factors associated with the presence or absence of job shifts. This essay is primarily focused on the adaptations that workers make to changes in employment opportunity, and its findings are drawn from their experience in selected industries or occupations in a metropolitan labor market. The groups chosen for intensive study were attached to industries or occupations that not only were of numerical importance in the Philadelphia labor market, but had undergone expansion or decline in whole or in part during the 10 years preceding the date of study in 1936. Some of the findings have been published previously, especially those on patterns of employment and unemployment during the decade from 1926 to 1936 as related to the earlier work history and personal characteristics of individuals.[1] The original work-history records and the tabulations for these studies have been re-examined for a retrospective view of how workers adapt to major changes in the structure of employment

[1] Gladys L. Palmer and Ada M. Stoflet, "The Labor Force of the Philadelphia Radio Industry in 1936," WPA National Research Project in co-operation with Industrial Research Department, University of Pennsylvania, *Report* No. P-2, Philadelphia, 1938. Helen Herrmann, "Ten Years of Work Experience of Philadelphia Machinists," WPA National Research Project in co-operation with Industrial Research Department, University of Pennsylvania, *Report* No. P-5, Philadelphia, 1938.

Gladys L. Palmer, et al., "Ten Years of Work Experience of Philadelphia Weavers and Loomfixers," WPA National Research Project in co-operation with Industrial Research Department, University of Pennsylvania, *Report* No. P-4, Philadelphia, 1938.

Gladys L. Palmer, "Mobility of Weavers in Three Textile Centers," *Quarterly Journal of Economics*, May 1941, pp. 460–487.

in a metropolitan community and the extent to which the findings support or differ from those of more recent studies with respect to factors in labor market behavior.

The Philadelphia economy is highly diversified, and the opportunity for workers to change jobs in a given occupation or grade of skill is relatively greater here than in less diversified communities. A large city presumably offers relatively more of such opportunity than a small city, but this assumption has never been tested. Nor do we know whether changes in the distribution of employment at given employment levels tend to offer more opportunity for job changes than do changes in employment levels. In any event, significant economic changes had occurred in the local economy of Philadelphia prior to 1936 that had the effect of reducing the total demand for workers in manufacturing industries relative to the population and of requiring or stimulating job shifts. A more detailed analysis of the character and reasons for these changes in the economy and their effect on the levels and distribution of total employment and the city's labor force will be published subsequently.[2]

For purposes of this essay, it may be noted that abnormally high levels of employment in shipbuilding and munitions industries during World War I were followed by rapid contraction and some shift in the relative importance of employment in heavy- and light-process metalworking plants in the area. The radio industry expanded in the early thirties, but it was one of the few local industries to expand during the depression period; relatively high levels of employment were also maintained in later years. In the twenties, there had been a rapid expansion of the full-fashioned hosiery industry to peak levels of employment in 1929, followed by irregularly declining levels of employment as some local plants moved to other locations or were not replaced when they went out of business. Employment in upholstery, carpet and rug, and woolen and worsted mills fluctuated during the twenties but had persistently declining levels in the thirties and even in the forties. Some plants in these industries were adversely affected by changes in consumption patterns; others moved to new locations or were not replaced when business failures occurred. Employment in the industries selected for study still accounts for a relatively high proportion of the total, and this city still has a relatively high share of national employment in these industries. Nevertheless, the competitive position of the city and its environs in these particular industries, with the exception

---

[2] The report to be published subsequently analyzes labor-force dynamics in relation to economic change in the Philadelphia labor market over recent decades.

of certain metal products, has been less advantageous than it was in earlier decades.

Workers Selected for Study. The data examined refer to (1) workers in all grades of skill for two industries of local importance that had expanded during the decade prior to 1936, namely, radio and full-fashioned hosiery manufacture, (2) to weavers and loomfixers in declining textile fabric industries, namely, upholstery goods, carpets, and woolen and worsted manufacture, and (3) to machinists and toolmakers, some of whom were attached to industries with contracting employment and others to industries with expanding employment.

For several of the situations studied, the year 1936 may be considered as a halfway point in the course of the economic developments that precipitated labor force changes. It was a more prosperous year than the years immediately preceding but less prosperous than some years in the twenties or than most years in the forties. For the particular groups of workers studied, the rate of unemployment reported in May 1936 was, in each case, lower than that for the city's workers generally. This difference may reflect the fact that many adaptations had already been made by the labor force of these industries and occupations to changes in the demand for labor. This is to say that collateral evidence indicates that some older male workers and some married women had become discouraged with job hunting after layoffs in the early thirties and had retired from the labor market by 1936. Others had moved out of the city or shifted to different types of work and no longer regarded the occupations and industries selected for study as their "usual" attachment; they were missed in the enumeration in 1936. Because the volume of total unemployment was relatively high in May 1936, the workers studied except in the case of radio workers were selected on the basis of reports of their usual occupation and current or usual industry, regardless of whether they were employed or unemployed when interviewed. Persons reporting a usual occupation but not seeking work in May 1936 were excluded. Radio workers were selected on the basis of current or recent employment in the radio industry. All persons in the Industrial Research Department's unemployment sample reporting the specified occupations and industries were interviewed for work histories in a follow-up survey, and complete life-work histories were obtained [3] for most of the workers

[3] For schedule and definitions, see publications cited in footnote 1. In addition to the factual data obtained on the schedule, narrative reports incorporated unguided comments in answer to these questions: How did you happen to get into this "trade"? How were most of your jobs obtained?

studied. Experience at all the city's large plants (including government establishments) and in most of the small plants in the industries concerned is reflected in the 2462 work records reviewed in this analysis.

Except for the radio industry, most of the workers studied were either attached to a skilled craft or engaged in highly specialized machine operations that required a considerable learning period. The weavers worked on products made on Jacquard looms or on looms with special attachments that required more skill and experience than weaving on the ordinary box loom. Full-fashioned knitters also worked on machines requiring experience and knowledge of how to make machine adjustments; women employed in this industry are less skilled than men, but more skilled than the average woman in factory employment. The machinists and toolmakers studied showed apprenticeship training on their records or were employed in plants that required the equivalent of such training. In the radio industry, on the other hand, only 28% of the men were skilled craftsmen and the rest of the workers were engaged in operations that required a short learning period. About two-thirds of the radio and textile workers interviewed were union members in 1936, but the number of machinists interviewed who were union members was relatively small.[4]

The samples may therefore have a larger proportion of skilled craftsmen or workers affiliated with trade unions than are found in the other studies discussed in this volume. The four studies reviewed here present contrasting types of labor market situations in 1936. The characteristics of radio and hosiery workers reflected relatively recent recruitment to expanding industries in the community. The workers were predominantly young and native-born, with relatively short work histories and a concentrated type of experience. (Table 1.) Weavers and loomfixers and machinists and toolmakers, on the other hand, were older, more experienced, with a higher proportion of their numbers born abroad, and a greater variety of experience on jobs. Although the proportion of single workers was higher among women than men in these samples, it was lower than the proportion for all women workers in the city. If the experience of these groups is typical, local metal-

---

[4] Union affiliation was not determined by a direct question. Radio and hosiery workers were classified as union or non-union in terms of the contract status of the mill, of current job of the employed, and the last job of the unemployed. At the date of study, all upholstery weavers were unionized and some weavers in the other textile industries were union members. Union affiliation was noted on the schedule if the information was volunteered.

TABLE 1. SELECTED PERSONAL AND WORK EXPERIENCE CHARACTERISTICS,
PHILADELPHIA WORK HISTORY STUDIES, 1936

Personal and Work Experience Characteristics	Usual Industry and/or Occupation in 1936					
	Radio Industry *		Full-Fashioned Hosiery Industry		Weavers and Loom-fixers †	Machin-ists and Tool-makers (Men)
	Men	Women	Knitters and Helpers (Men)	Toppers, Loopers, Seamers (Women)		
Total in sample	421	265	412	324	357	683
Median age in 1936	32.7	24.3	29.6	27.2	44.5	45.2
Median years of schooling	8.6	8.9	8.5	8.4	7.8	8.4
Per cent single	32.8	57.7	30.3	46.9	19.4	11.3
Per cent foreign-born	28.5	9.1	10.8	16.7	38.7	33.0
Median years at usual occupation	6.9	3.1	9.7	7.9	18.5	22.5
Median months at longest job	55.2	32.4	45.9	49.1	111.6	122.4
Per cent entered labor market 1926–1936	30.3	65.3	27.2	42.3	6.5	6.1
Per cent with less than 10 years' residence in Philadelphia	9.5	8.3	4.9	4.3	5.3	11.8

Source: Reports cited in text footnote 1 and unpublished materials in the Industrial Research Department's files.

* Radio workers were employed in the radio industry in May 1936, or, if unemployed, this was the industry of their most recent job.

† Predominantly men. Usual industry: upholstery, carpets and rugs, and woolen and worsted goods.

products industries had attracted more skilled workers from outside the city in the period from 1926 to 1936 than was the case for textile workers.

Workers of foreign birth were predominantly from England and Scotland in the case of weavers and loomfixers. The specialized types of fabrics woven in Philadelphia had attracted workers from the textile centers of the British Isles from the very beginnings of the textile industries in this area, and even after World War I workers continued to come to the area. Foreign-born workers in full-fashioned hosiery manufacture, on the other hand, were predominantly from Germany and Poland. Radio workers of foreign birth included a significant number of Italian cabinetmakers who had transferred from cabinet work on victrolas to the finishing of radio cabinets. Machinists and toolmakers of foreign birth had come predominantly from Germany and Great Britain, and many had served their apprenticeship terms abroad. But the majority of workers in all four studies were native-born and the vast majority, whether native-born or foreign-born, had lived in Philadelphia for a relatively long period of time.

Selected mobility measures for the decade from 1926 through 1936 are presented in Table 2. In judging these measures, it should be

TABLE 2.   JOB SEPARATIONS AND WORK EXPERIENCE, 1926–1935, PHILADELPHIA WORK HISTORY STUDIES, 1936

Job Separations and Experience, 1926–1935	Radio		Full-Fashioned Hosiery		Weavers and Loom-fixers	Machin-ists and Tool-makers
	Men	Women	Men	Women		
Total job separations *	1516	651 †	1623	812	929	1585
Per cent distribution	100.0	100.0	100.0	100.0	100.0	100.0
Separations to unemployment ‡	3.4	8.4	4.3	4.9	10.2	3.5
Return to same job	26.4	29.7	21.7	22.9	22.0	19.6
Separations involving shifts §	70.2	61.9	74.0	72.2	67.8	76.9
Employer	6.9	6.8	37.5	44.0	25.8	8.7
Employer and occupation	2.8	3.7	5.1	3.8	2.8	1.8
Employer and industry	11.2	1.7	0.4	0.2	5.5	29.9
Occupation	9.6	8.1	12.2	7.2	4.3	6.0
Other combinations	39.7	41.6	18.8	17.0	29.4	30.5
Median number of separations per worker	3.5	2.7	4.2	2.7	2.5	2.2
Per cent of workers with no job separations	6.4	15.5	5.5	15.1	10.4	26.2
Median length of jobs at usual occupation (months)	22.5	14.6	23.9	27.1	36.9	44.5
Per cent distribution of average man-months (rounded)	100.0	100.0	100.0	100.0	100.0	100.0
Employed						
At usual occupation	38.7 ‖	30.7 ‖	58.4	60.4	64.6	70.7
At other occupations	29.6 ¶	11.0 ¶	22.0	7.6	16.1	15.2
Unemployed	17.3	15.5	10.7	8.1	15.7	11.2
Not seeking work						
Before entering labor market	13.7	34.0	7.2	14.9	2.4	2.1
After entering labor market	0.7	8.8	1.7	9.0	1.2	0.8

* Involving 1 month or more of unemployment or time not seeking work.
† Excludes 55 separations for which type of shift was not available.
‡ Unemployed as of December 1935. Does not include persons whose unemployment was followed by return to same job by December 1935.
§ Excludes in-grade promotions.
‖ Refers to time employed in radio industry.
¶ Refers to time employed in industries other than radio.

noted that the degree of exposure as well as of employment opportunity differed among the groups studied. Radio workers may more readily be compared with hosiery workers, and weavers and loomfixers with machinists and toolmakers, for these two pairs of groups had approximately the same degree of exposure to the labor market. When one analyzes the types of job shifts made during this decade, employer shifts were a significant part of the total for hosiery workers and weavers but were not significant for the other two groups, for whom employer shifts were usually combined with occupational or industrial shifts. Multiple-type shifts were characteristic of the 10-year experience of a substantial proportion of workers in each group. Over a fourth of the machinists and toolmakers reported no job separations during this period, but this proportion was much lower in the other groups studied. Associated with this feature of the experience of machinists and toolmakers is a relatively high average length of service per job at the usual occupation during the decade. In general, the jobs held during this decade were much shorter than the longest jobs recorded for these workers (Table 1) and shorter than the average length of service reported by all persons in the city's labor force in 1938.[5] Although there were some differences in exposure between men and women in the radio and hosiery industries, men reported more job separations than women and there were relatively fewer men than women with no job separations (Table 2).

Recruitment to Expanding Industries. When major changes occur in the industrial distribution of employment in a community, the usual channel by which such changes are effectuated is the recruitment of young persons to expanding industries. As older workers in contracting industries leave, they are not replaced. If contraction takes place too rapidly, however, or occurs during a depression when total employment levels are low, a substantial number of workers are displaced and join the ranks of the unemployed. This was the situation in Philadelphia during the thirties. One of the initial objectives of the radio study was to see if any workers displaced from contracting industries had succeeded in getting employment in the one local industry that had expanded during the depression. It was found that a substantial proportion of radio workers had been recruited directly from school and that most of those who had transferred to this industry from declining industries were a selected group from the point of

[5] The median length of service on the current job reported by employed persons in 1938 was 8.3 years for men and 4.8 years for women. Gladys L. Palmer assisted by Samuel M. Cohn, "Employment and Unemployment in Philadelphia, July-August, 1938," *Industrial Research Department Special Report* No. 7, Philadelphia, 1939, page 16.

view of age. That is to say, they were younger than the average
worker in the declining industries in the city.[6]

Some workers started in the radio industry because it was the only
industry with job openings when they entered the labor market. For
a few experienced workers, employment in radio was a stop-gap activity, as they expected to return to previous types of jobs "when things
picked up." Others with limited experience indicated reasons similar to
those of one man who said that "radio was just starting up at this time
and everybody was going there." Still others had "tinkered" with radio
sets at home or taken special training courses and wanted this particular type of experience. They had haunted the personnel offices or
stood in lines at the gates until they had secured jobs. As a result, the
radio work force in 1936 reflected the recruitment of a large number
of recent school and college graduates, supplemented by experienced
workers from a wide variety of manufacturing and nonmanufacturing
industries. Although most radio workers had secured jobs through
friends and relatives, there were more instances of placements through
public employment office and school channels than for some of the
other groups studied. This difference reflects the relatively recent
development of such public services on a broad scale.

Experienced workers who transferred to full-fashioned hosiery manufacture had also come from a wide variety of the city's industries, but
chiefly manufacturing.[7] Here too, however, a relatively large proportion
had been recruited directly from school although not from college. The
outstanding influence noted in the comments of hosiery workers about
why they were attracted to this industry was its reputation for high
earnings. During the expansion of this industry, earnings, as a result
of a relatively high wage scale and a substantial amount of overtime
work, were sufficiently high [8] to merit public attention in a community
where the average earnings of factory workers are lower than in other
cities of comparable size. Knowledge of what industries are high-
wage or low-wage industries appears to be common in a metropolitan
labor market. Like the other groups studied, the majority of hosiery
workers had secured jobs through relatives or friends or by direct appli-

[6] Palmer and Stoflet, *op. cit.*, p. 51.

[7] Findings cited for hosiery workers, except as otherwise noted, came from unpublished materials in the files of the Industrial Research Department.

[8] In 1929, median annual earnings of full-time workers in union hosiery mills
were as follows: legging, $3237; footing, $3965; topping, $1346; looping, $1289;
seaming, $1239. George W. Taylor, *The Full-Fashioned Hosiery Worker*, Univer-
sity of Pennsylvania Press, 1931, p. 96.

cation. It was an unusual case when a hosiery worker indicated that there were no members of his or her family or relatives who were not also employed in this industry. Many schedules reflected the comment of one knitter who said that the "hosiery trade runs in my family."

When intermittent operations became more characteristic of the hosiery industry and a declining trend in local employment became apparent, the workers still maintained a strong sense of attachment to the industry. This attitude persisted despite the necessity of taking wage cuts during the depression and of making adjustments to a series of technological changes.[9] The strong sense of attachment to the industry was reflected in an incident that occurred in 1940. Special defense retraining programs were developed for unemployed knitters with the active co-operation of the union in several cities, including Philadelphia. It was the hope of the union that knitters by reason of their knowledge of machine adjustments might be placed in the munitions industries, either on machine-operating or repair and adjustment jobs. But at the end of this program, as one union official ruefully remarked, the knitters applied for work as "knitters" rather than as "machine-operators" or "machine-adjusters." Nevertheless, many knitters and workers from other hosiery occupations did secure jobs in munitions industries during the war and have not returned to the hosiery industry.

Experience in a Contracting Occupation—Weavers. Despite the fact that the rate of unemployment for weavers and loomfixers was lower than the average rate in the city in 1936, the incidence of long-term unemployment was high for this group, as for other workers displaced from industries subject to a downward trend. Moreover, such depression jobs as were obtained by displaced weavers typically represented a downgrading in skill class. The records for upholstery and woolen and worsted weavers, and to a lesser extent for carpet weavers, show one or more decades of movement from the weaving of one type of fabric to another as changing consumption patterns and other economic changes modified the relative importance of various local products. A decline in employment for all types of locally made fabrics was an unforeseen development in the relatively long experience of Philadelphia weavers. Their skills were more specialized and not readily transferable to other industries. Their comments comparing textile jobs with those held in other industries, particularly during

[9] These changes included the development of finer gauges and higher speeds in knitting equipment, the introduction of nylon in place of silk, and the introduction of the single-unit machine which eliminated the operation of topping.

World War I, indicate a preference for "light" work or work on fabrics. Although their earnings were low during the thirties because of short-time operations and intermittent layoffs, they stuck by their looms. Those without a job attachment, who had "pounded the pavements" looking for work after layoffs, were at a loss as to what to try next. Weavers, like hosiery workers, came from families where sons and daughters followed their parents in working in textile mills, and they, too, resided in the neighborhoods of the mills. For many weavers, the textile industry was the largest or the only industry in the communities in which they had grown up, either in this country or abroad. For those born and raised in the textile district of Philadelphia, the textile industry was the only one they knew intimately. They entered it because their families or friends urged it, because the work was located near their homes, or because they or their families knew the foremen and superintendents of the mills who could help them secure jobs, if jobs were scarce.

From the long-run point of view, the weavers in Philadelphia were better off than those in such single-industry communities as Manchester, New Hampshire, or Paterson, New Jersey, in 1936. Several points may be noted in this connection.[10] Philadelphia weavers were younger, they had had better schooling than weavers in the other two cities, and their experience was much more varied. Moreover, the proportion of persons entering the Philadelphia labor market as weavers in the decade from 1926 to 1936 was smaller than a like proportion in the other two cities. This difference lends support to the view that old industries decline more rapidly in a diversified than in a highly specialized manufacturing center. In specialized centers without alternative opportunities for employment, the continued entrance of young people to a declining industry tends to render the inevitable transitions more difficult. In 1936, the chances were that, if a policy of few or no replacements to the work force were followed, Philadelphia weavers might weather the storm, although there would be casualties. In effect, this was what happened, and the process was aided by the movement of some textile workers to other industries during World War II and post-war years.

Machinists and Toolmakers. The proportion of recent entrants to the labor market as machinists and toolmakers or apprentices to these occupations in 1936 was even smaller than for weavers. As events developed, it was too small to meet the demand in these occupations

---

[10] Palmer, *Quarterly Journal of Economics, op. cit.,* pp. 467, 471–472.

in the late thirties and ridiculously small in the face of defense and war production demands in the forties. During World War II, this situation was remedied by recruitment of more apprentices, extensive job dilution, and special training programs. What is of more interest for the purposes of this analysis is the experience of machinists between the close of World War I and 1936.

Rapid declines in employment followed the cancellation of war contracts after World War I, which were more pronounced in transportation equipment than in other industries, although most metal-products industries in the area were affected initially. In addition, the naval disarmament program and the shifting of foreign commerce to foreign carriers further reduced the demand for labor in private shipyards and the Philadelphia Navy Yard. One large shipyard and one steel plant in the city closed during the twenties and were not reopened until World War II. There were changes also in the location of establishments engaged in locomotive building and railroad equipment repair during this period. Moreover, although plants in the Philadelphia area had done a considerable amount of experimental work and continued to make parts for the relatively new automobile industry during the twenties, the chief center of that industry developed elsewhere. At a later date, the expansion of the aircraft engine industry also by-passed this area except for small segments. The only local metal-products industries that increased substantially after World War I were the industries producing electrical machinery and supplies, particularly radios and television. All of these industries and the substantial machinery industry (other than electrical) employ machinists and toolmakers.

It was the opinion of personnel officers during the period under review that the machinists who had been employed in transportation equipment manufacture and in plants with heavier types of processing could not meet the specifications for precision work in lighter-process plants and that they therefore would have difficulty in making such a shift. An attempt was made to test this hypothesis for 466 men classified as machinists in 1936 who were also in the labor market in 1917–1918. For men who became machinists by 1936 but were not in the labor market in World War I, it may be said at once that they were recruited to light-process plants in larger numbers than to the heavier industries where employment was declining. This recruitment policy, which affected all occupations, had the effect of creating a differential in the average age of workers in heavy-process as compared with light-process metal industries by 1936. Younger men predominated in the latter type of work in all grades of skill, including machinists.

What happened to the older machinists? To answer this question, the status of this group of machinists in 1926, a prosperous year about halfway between World War I and 1936, was compared with their status in 1917–1918. The employment of machinists, as reflected by the experience of this group, was greater in heavy-process than in light-process plants in 1926, although not so high as during World War I.[11] About 38% of the total in the labor market at both dates were with the same employer in 1926 as in 1917–1918, and they constituted the oldest single group among these machinists. About a fourth of the machinists in the labor market at both dates had shifted employers but remained in the same broad type of metal processing or continued as maintenance machinists in nonmetal industries. In the course of major shifts by 176 machinists, light-process plants gained more than they lost and maintenance work in nonmetal industries gained, but the reverse was true for heavy-process industries. The machinists who made these shifts were younger than those making no shifts.

This evidence with respect to the difficulties in shifting from heavy to light work is not conclusive. Some of the younger machinists apparently made satisfactory shifts, and the comments of those displaced from the heavy industries during the twenties indicate no feeling that their experience was a particular handicap in securing a job during that period. By 1936, however, there was a relatively heavy representation among unemployed machinists of men whose usual industry had been transportation equipment and other types of heavy processing. Moreover, machinists from these industries had experienced more unemployment over the decade from 1926 to 1936 than those from other industries.[12] If a similar type of analysis could be made for World War II and post-war experience, the limits to the transferability of machinists' skills, if they exist in any substantial degree in fact, might be more rigorously stated.

Another finding concerns a difference in the experience patterns of machinists and toolmakers. In an unpublished study of the work experience of men in the Philadelphia metal-working crafts made after

---

[11] Of the 466 men classified as machinists in 1936 who were in the labor market in 1917–1918, 360 were in the metal-products industries at the earlier date, 290 were engaged as machinists, and 70 as apprentices and machine operators; 30 were maintenance machinists in nonmetal industries; 42 were in other occupations; and 34 in military service.

[12] Helen Herrmann, *op. cit.*, p. 72.

World War I and substantiated in the records just cited that were obtained in 1936, it was found that, whereas Philadelphia machinists frequently stay in the plants in which their apprenticeship is served, toolmakers seldom, if ever, do so. Moreover, instances of a machinist spending his entire working life at the plant where he served his apprenticeship are not uncommon. In Philadelphia, toolmakers shift from product to product or plant to plant to secure a broader experience and the knowledge that they consider necessary for proficiency in the occupation. It may be noted that some production machinists also took this view. As one man said, "By going to several places after you finish your apprenticeship you soon find out if you should stay in the trade." The moderate size of Philadelphia plants or the organization of local metal-products industries may account for this pattern. If, as is likely, it exists on a wider geographic scale, it indicates the possible presence of specific patterns of job changes in the skilled crafts. If workers can secure all the experience that they believe is needed for proficiency in the occupation without changing their place of employment or gaining experience in the processing of a diversity of products, there will be relatively few such shifts; otherwise they will tend to make industrial and possibly geographic shifts. Not only therefore will the job records for occupations differ, but the differences will tend to reflect the patterns in which experience is believed to be gained in each occupation.

Every type of machinist was represented in this survey. The itinerant type was well represented by a Peruvian for whom almost every job change was reported "to see the country"; he had worked his way from Peru to Philadelphia and from there to Chicago and back as a machinist. Others said that they were "restless" or "liked to change jobs every year." There were "jobbing machinists," who had stayed in the city but had worked on special orders in so many places that they could not remember their names and were always "in and out of work." At the other extreme were men who had secured what they considered "good" jobs and stayed on them for long periods of time. All grades of skill were represented in the course of the machinists' work records, from foremen, machine erectors and lay-out men, first- and second-class production machinists, and maintenance machinists, to apprentices, helpers, and machine operators.

The machinists had entered the occupation for all kinds of reasons. As might be expected, the records of more of the machinists and toolmakers than of the other groups studied yielded evidence of mechanical aptitudes or a definite preference for work with machinery. Some men came from families with experience and interest in the metal-working crafts, as in the case of one who said: "There was a lathe, a drill press, and a shaper in our cellar and as soon as we were big enough to reach the handle on the drill press, we started to learn the trade." Yet not all machinists were in this group. In fact, the majority might be said to have gotten into the trade by "accident," so far as the available data indicate reasons for occupational choice. That some even disliked the work is reflected in these comments: "I certainly did not learn the machinists' trade because I liked it; this was what I was doing when I got married and had to settle down." "My father said I had to learn a trade or he'd break my neck, and this was it." Some men became interested in work on machinery while serving in the Army or Navy or taking vocational school training. Many more were influenced to shift from other jobs to take the time out for apprenticeship training by relatives, neighbors, and friends, whose opinion about employment prospects they respected.

Despite the predominance of what on the surface appear to be accidental factors in occupational choice for machinists, their work records show purposeful pursuit of the occupation, once started. They quit jobs to get "more experience," "more money," or a "better" job. If laid off, they picked up odd jobs until they were "called back" or secured other attachments. Sometimes, what looked like a "better" job at the time did not turn out to be so, particularly during the depression, and regrets concerning the change were occasionally expressed. On the whole, however, the records show a rational explanation of job shifts in terms of the age and experience of the worker in relation to changes in employment levels and in the demand for machinists in different local industries.

Although most jobs held by Philadelphia machinists had been obtained through relatives and friends or by direct application, some use of employment offices was indicated. In a metropolitan community where many types of industries use machinists there is need for a centralized hiring channel. The public employment offices, vocational schools, and the local metal manufacturers' association performed such services.

The general comments and reasons noted for changing jobs on the part of machinists reveal strong opinions about working conditions in the labor market. Some workers liked to work in the big plants because they had engineering departments and were constantly developing new products. Others liked the small places "where you knew everybody" and had some variety in assignments. The high spot of one machinist's career is reflected in the comment: "I helped to cut almost every gear that operates the Gatun locks." Many machinists had definite opinions as to which plants offered the best "all-round" apprenticeship training and in which plants the training was too specialized. They commented that in some plants the work was "hard" but offered "good money" and, in others, there was "too much supervision." Those who had been embittered by long periods of unemployment during the depression tended to blame the "specialists for spoiling the machinists' trade," the foreign-trained workers, for whom they alleged that employers had a hiring preference, the hiring practices that discriminated against older men, or the "sweatshop tactics" of jobbing machine shops in respect to wages. The knowledge of the labor market revealed by machinists may or may not have been completely accurate, but there is no evidence of general ignorance or apathy in the opinions volunteered in the course of interviews.

Generalizations. Certain generalizations may be drawn from the experience of these four groups of Philadelphia workers. One is that the recruitment to expanding industries of inexperienced workers just out of school and of younger workers among those with experience results in a differentiation in the age composition of expanding and contracting industries. When the average age of workers in contracting industries is high, it has the effect of increasing the rate of retirement, and, if few or no replacements are made, the adjustments will be more rapid. If permanent layoffs occur, the specific risks of long-term unemployment or of forced retirement are likely to be suffered by the oldest workers affected. One would not wish to minimize the character of the problems created under these circumstances, but it may be noted that they are clear-cut and can be more readily attacked.

When one looks at lifetime work histories, older workers have a more varied experience than younger workers because of differences in exposure. With the same exposure, however, as for any given five- or ten-year period in the labor market, younger workers make more shifts of employer, occupation, or industry, or all three, than older workers, and men are more mobile than women. The mobility patterns also vary. With approximately the same exposure, a majority of hosiery workers, for example, changed employers but stayed in the same industry, whereas radio workers made multiple-type shifts. Weavers also changed employers frequently, whereas machinists and toolmakers with approximately the same exposure seldom changed employers without changing industry.

Labor mobility responds to opportunity. There were more voluntary shifts and more successful types of shifts in the first half of the decade from 1926 to 1935 than in the latter half. In a depression the labor force is less mobile, and such movement as takes place is largely involuntary. Downgrading of skill, unemployment, and retirement from the labor market are likely to accompany the job separations that occur during a depression. In this connection, it was found in one study of workers laid off from 3 Philadelphia hosiery mills in 1933 that the worker with varied experience is less handicapped in securing another job than one with more specialized experience. The worker with experience in only one establishment, for example, is protected by seniority rights as long as his employer stays in business, but is handicapped in securing other work if his employer goes out of business.[13] The desirability of long service with one employer has for many years been accepted by Philadelphia employers and workers. This acceptance may flow from the fact that the city has had many relatively long-lived business establishments and a relatively mature labor force with certain traditional attitudes. Whether the experience of the depression and war years has undermined these traditions and whether relatively long periods of service on jobs are equally characteristic of cities located in other regions or with differing industrial and occupational structures are not known.

One gains the impression from a review of the Philadelphia work history records that the workers concerned had a considerable knowledge of labor market conditions and pursued their occupational careers in a purposeful fashion, even though seemingly "accidental" factors affected the decision to accept jobs or the choice of occupations, in the first instance. Over time, a process of "accommodation" appears to take place in which a worker's initial vocational aspirations are adjusted to the economic realities of the job market in his community and are increasingly restricted to a consideration of opportunities in the occupation or industry in which he finds that he has some proficiency and to which he considers himself attached. The work record over time may therefore reflect more consistent and purposeful movement than the activities at any particular point in time. Even a high degree of immobility represented in a lifetime of experience in a single plant is not necessarily the result of ignorance or irrational behavior.

[13] Gladys L. Palmer and Constance Williams, "Reemployment of Philadelphia Hosiery Workers after Shut-Downs in 1933–1934," WPA National Research Project in co-operation with Industrial Research Department, University of Pennsylvania, *Report* No. P-6, Philadelphia, 1939, p. 45.

A parallel approach may be suggested for the hiring side of job transactions. In any given year, the hiring preferences or practices of an employer may be relaxed or made more stringent by reason of the size of the labor reserve and the qualifications of current job applicants. Over the years, however, a work force is recruited to an establishment that reflects a process of "accommodation" by the employer to the type of workers available in the community who show some disposition to remain with the company. The characteristics of the total work force may therefore bear little resemblance to the hiring specifications in use at a particular point of time.

If the generalized findings noted in this essay appear to be restricted in number and only indirectly related to any explanation of labor market behavior, this impression is explained not only by the fact that a comprehensive program of direct measurement of attitudes was not undertaken in the Philadelphia studies, but also because the workers studied reveal significant differences in behavior, as measured by what they did as well as by what they said. These differences appear to be related to the occupational or industrial environment of workers and the effect on them of cyclical influences in the time period covered, in addition to such personal characteristics as sex, age, or marital status. It follows from this position that the writer would support Myers' suggestion (in Chapter 5) concerning the "fallacy of attempting any universal generalizations on 'what workers want in jobs.'"

Corroboration of Findings of More Recent Studies. The statistical data and narratives obtained in connection with the Philadelphia studies of 1936 support the findings of more recent studies in New England communities [14] with respect to several considerations. In general, the Philadelphia workers studied secured most of their jobs through relatives and friends or by direct application to plants. The first jobs held, jobs held during a war (except in the metal-working crafts), and jobs held after a permanent layoff during a severe depression, bore less relation to the rest of the work records than other jobs. If one excludes these types of experience from consideration, the Philadelphia workers studied, like most workers in other cities, show a strong sense of attachment to a given occupation or industry.

[14] Lloyd G. Reynolds and Joseph Shister, *Job Horizons,* Harper, New York, 1949, and Reynolds, *The Structure of Labor Markets,* Harper, New York, 1951.

Charles A. Myers and W. Rupert Maclaurin, *The Movement of Factory Workers.* The Technology Press and John Wiley & Sons, New York, 1943.

Charles A. Myers and George P. Shultz, *The Dynamics of a Labor Market,* Prentice-Hall, New York, 1951.

No attempt was made to test directly the degree of knowledge Philadelphia workers had about the labor market or about wages and working conditions in local plants. Nevertheless, the data obtained substantiate Reynolds and Shister's comment to the effect that skilled workers and union workers have a considerable knowledge of conditions in their industry.[15] This finding can be tested best in the case of (Philadelphia) textile workers. Unionized hosiery workers, for example, worked under a standard piecework scale in 1936 and non-union plants in the area had comparable wage scales. Earnings under these scales, however, varied from plant to plant with the type of product or equipment and the efficiency of the enterprise. Full-fashioned hosiery knitters evidently had information concerning the plants that provided an opportunity for the best earnings, because many shifts between plants on identical work were reported to secure a "better machine," a "better job," or "more wages."

Upholstery weavers also worked under a standard piecework scale, and here, too, earnings differed between local plants by reason of differences in regularity of operation, type of fabric made, and in age and condition of the looms. The union records of 1926 and 1927, analyzed by Dr. Anne Bezanson,[16] and the work histories obtained in 1936 indicate a considerable movement of weavers from plant to plant, with the objective of obtaining higher earnings through "steadier work" or "better looms." The significance of these findings with respect to their implications about knowledge of the labor market may best be expressed by citing Dr. Bezanson's finding: [17]

Further there is indicated a considerable knowledge on the part of workers of conditions and working opportunity in the trade. How far this knowledge is due to the specialized skill of the occupation, the organization of the craft, or the moderate size of the industry, is unknown.

All the factors noted undoubtedly influence the knowledge of workers about work opportunity and the job market. Further research is needed to amplify these findings if, in fact, limitation of knowledge about the job market is found to retard the mobility of labor.

In their preliminary report, Reynolds and Shister found that union workers were less mobile than non-union workers, a finding they at-

[15] Lloyd G. Reynolds and Joseph Shister, *op. cit.*, p. 47.

[16] Anne Bezanson, *Earnings and Working Opportunity in the Upholstery Weavers Trade in 25 Plants in Philadelphia*. University of Pennsylvania Press, 1928.

[17] Anne Bezanson, "The Advantages of Labor Turnover: An Illustrative Case," *Quarterly Journal of Economics*, May 1928, p. 464.

tributed in part to a difference in length of service between the two groups.[18] In the Philadelphia studies, there was an opportunity to check differences in the mobility of union and non-union workers in the full-fashioned hosiery industry, where approximately half of the sample was union and half non-union.[19] The only significant difference between union and non-union hosiery workers in Philadelphia in 1936 was a 2-year difference in the average age of knitters, or what may be assumed to be a 2-year difference in the dates at which they entered the labor market. In the occupations employing women, the average age was approximately the same for both union and non-union workers. In contrast to the findings for a New England city, union hosiery workers in Philadelphia tended to make more shifts of employer, occupation, or industry in the 10 years from 1926 to 1936 than non-union workers, although this difference in mobility is not significant when workers in each occupation are considered separately. Findings of the Philadelphia studies would support the view that occupational differences outweigh considerations of union membership as a factor in the mobility of workers in a given industry or community.

Despite the fact that Reynolds and Shister make the necessary qualifications in interpreting the data that they collected in 1947, one gains the impression from reading *Job Horizons* that accidental factors play a significant part in single job transactions in a given period of time such as 1 year, and that the planning of a career or purposeful movement from job to job are luxuries not indulged in by the average manual worker. This is not the general impression one gains from the Philadelphia studies of 1936, where the analysis stresses five- and ten-year periods or a lifetime experience. It is possible that the existence of more plants and branches of any given industry in a metropolitan city offers more opportunity to test factors in movement than are found in

[18] Reynolds and Shister, *op. cit.*, pp. 48–49. This finding has been modified as a result of later analysis along the lines suggested by evidence from the Philadelphia studies.

[19] It is probable that more than half of the full-fashioned hosiery workers in the city were members of the union in 1936. One of the School Blocks in the Industrial Research Department unemployment sample happened to be located near the largest plant in the city, which was, at that time, not organized. Many workers in this plant, as in other hosiery mills, lived near the plant, and the total hosiery sample is somewhat overweighted by workers from this particular mill. Despite this bias in the sample, there is no reason to believe that the work histories of union as opposed to non-union workers in the sample are not representative of the work histories of these two groups in the industry.

a smaller city. It is also possible that the aftermath of a decade of
depression and a war may have permanently changed the character of
workers' attitudes with respect to the choice and pursuit of an occupational or industrial career. The dates of these studies differ but, if
anything, accidental factors should have been more apparent in work
records obtained in 1936 than in those obtained in 1947, to the extent
that the significance of accidental factors is related to a tendency of
unemployed workers to accept the first job offered.

Whether studies are made in years of prosperity or depression, it is
the opinion of the writer that career framework considerations outweigh accidental circumstances if one looks at the record of jobs *over
time,* as distinct from a cross-section view of a number of single job
transactions in a local market at any given time. For a variety of
reasons, accidental factors play a significant role in the choice of first
jobs, and such jobs may be a high proportion of the total number of
job transactions at any given time. For some workers who have no
major financial responsibilities or who would find it difficult to make
satisfactory work adjustments under any conditions, accidental factors
may play an important role throughout their work history, but they
are in a minority. For most workers in selected manufacturing industries of a metropolitan community like Philadelphia for the years preceding 1936, the experience records appear to have a rationale, and
what may be called "career framework" considerations explain many,
if not most, job changes. Economic considerations loom large in this
context. Workers quit jobs to get "steadier work," "more money,"
"better working conditions," "more experience," or what they consider
to be a "promotion." If they are forced to change jobs by layoffs, they
may have to accept any job that they can get, but their subsequent
history will show an attempt to return to the company or work that they
prefer or, occasionally, a permanent shift to a new type of work. For
the latter type of change, which represents a modification of their career plans, they give explanations that are reasonable to them in terms
of their qualifications and the character of job opportunities at the
time.

A single job transaction is one of a series and is likely to bear some
relationship to previous and prospective transactions. For this reason
the character of job transactions over time provides more effective clues
to behavior patterns or motivations than a cross-section view of job
transactions at any given time. Certainly our vocational training and
guidance and personnel and placement programs are off to a bad start

if most labor market transactions are the result of "accidental" forces, and "career framework" considerations are of minor importance in labor market behavior. The findings of current studies with respect to these considerations are so important for the policy decisions of public and private agencies that they should be checked and double-checked in as many types of situations as possible.

4. Labor Mobility in Two Communities

CHARLES A. MYERS

Professor of Industrial Relations and Director of the Industrial Relations Section Massachusetts Institute of Technology

Since 1940 there has been considerable interest in the movement of labor within a local labor market. This interest grew out of a dissatisfaction with the traditional assumptions of economic theory about the movement of workers from one job to another in response to differences in wage rates.[1] Until a number of university research centers turned their attention to local labor markets, there was inadequate information on the amount, direction, and incentives for and effects of the movement of workers within a typical industrial community. There are still serious gaps in our knowledge of labor mobility, but a beginning has been made in answering the questions that are basic for adequate understanding of the labor market and for intelligent policies affecting mobility of workers.

The Industrial Relations Section at the Massachusetts Institute of Technology has conducted two local labor market studies, one in 1937–1942 and one during 1948–1949. The first was an analysis of the movement of factory workers in two adjacent, industrially diversified Massachusetts cities, with a 1940 population of about 64,000. The second study was made in a New Hampshire city of 35,000, where a large textile mill closed a substantial portion of its operations late in 1948, displacing more than 1700 workers. It is the purpose of this essay to indicate the central findings of these two studies, in the light of their somewhat different objectives, and to suggest significant conclusions of labor mobility which grow out of these and other local labor market

[1] An example of the traditional line of thought is the following: "The movement of labour from place to place is insufficient to iron out local differences in wages. But the movement does occur, and recent researches are indicating more and more clearly that differences in net economic advantages, chiefly differences in wages, are the main causes of migration." (J. R. Hicks, *The Theory of Wages*, The Macmillan Co., London, 1932, p. 76.)

68

studies. A final section will deal with limitations of our two studies, and unanswered questions for further research.

OBJECTIVES OF THE TWO STUDIES

The first study, in 1937–1942, was based on an analysis of the employment and earnings records of nearly 16,000 workers employed at some time during 1937–1939 by 37 firms representing three-fourths of the factory employment in the community. Answers were sought to the following questions: (1) What proportion of factory workers have fairly steady employment throughout the year? (2) What proportion move between firms, and how much of this movement is voluntary? (3) What are the characteristics of the workers who move voluntarily from one job to another? (4) In what directions does most movement take place—to similar firms and jobs, up or down the occupational ladder? (5) Do high-wage firms attract workers while low-wage firms lose them? (6) What are the principal barriers to mobility in a local labor market?

The second study, in 1948–1949, had somewhat different objectives and concerned a different group of workers—a random-number sample of 51 textile workers who left voluntarily after the shutdown announcement and a sample of 144 of the much larger group which was laid off subsequently as mill operations were curtailed. Another part of the study, not directly relevant to labor mobility, concerned the impact of this unemployment on the personnel and wage policies of the other firms and unions in the community.

In the mobility part of this second study, we were interested in the following questions, among others: (1) What are the characteristics of the more mobile group which left voluntarily as compared to those who remained with the firm until they were laid off? (2) How do displaced workers go about finding other jobs? (3) How much information do they have about available jobs? (4) What factors or job satisfactions attract them to certain jobs rather than to others; how important are wages and other "economic" attractions relative to non-economic attractions? The last three questions were directly related to an earlier study by the Labor and Management Center at Yale University, and an effort was made to test the hypotheses advanced in that study.[2]

[2] Lloyd G. Reynolds and Joseph Shister, *Job Horizons*, Harper, New York, 1949. The Yale study was later expanded in the final report by Reynolds, *The Structure of Labor Markets*, Harper, New York, 1951.

PRINCIPAL FINDINGS OF FIRST STUDY

A full report of the 1937–1942 labor market study has been published elsewhere,[3] and the principal results relating to labor mobility may be summarized as follows:

1. Of the 16,000 workers in the sample, 71% did not have continuous employment with one of the 37 principal manufacturing firms in the community during the three years 1937–1939. Only 14% of these had jobs in more than one of the 37 firms; the great majority were either unemployed, in other occupations, or out of the labor market during parts of those 3 years.

2. About 30% of the moves among the 37 firms were voluntary; the rest of the moves were forced by layoffs or discharges. During a period of some unemployment, therefore, only a minority of the workers were willing or able to quit their jobs because they were dissatisfied or because they had found a better job. More than a fourth of the voluntary moves were for family, personal, or physical reasons.

3. Workers who moved voluntarily were usually young, short-service workers, frequently women, who were relatively low-paid in the jobs that they quit. Workers who left one firm voluntarily and then stayed only a short time in the next firm before quitting constituted the small "active fringe" of mobile workers (less than a fifth of those who moved voluntarily), and there were proportionately more young, single men in this group.

4. Workers tended to seek and accept jobs within their immediate neighborhoods, largely because they learned of openings or secured jobs through the influence of employed friends and relatives. These neighborhood clusters of movement coincided in part with the fact that similar firms were located in these areas. For example, there were several plastics, apparel, paper products, and furniture firms in one section of the local labor market, and in another, three shoe and leather products firms were close to two cotton yarn mills and a metal products firm. Most of the voluntary movement was within these clusters, and considerably less movement occurred between them and other firms, even though there were some job opportunities elsewhere.

[3] Charles A. Myers and W. Rupert Maclaurin, *The Movement of Factory Workers,* The Technology Press and John Wiley & Sons, New York, 1943, and two articles by the authors, "After Unemployment Benefits Are Exhausted," *Quarterly Journal of Economics, 56,* Feb. 1942, pp. 231–255, and "The Movement of Factory Labor and Its Relation to Wages," *ibid., 57,* Feb. 1943, pp. 241–264.

Workers either did not know of alternative job opportunities in the other cluster and in outside firms, or they were unwilling to commute longer distances to work.[4] Possibly if job opportunities elsewhere had been rapidly expanding in 1937–1939, these neighborhood clusters of movement would have broken down.

5. More than a third of the voluntary moves during 1937–1939 resulted in lower earnings, but one-half earned more on the new job than on the job that they left. Some movement occurred in the direction of higher-wage firms, although it was not very great. There was little evidence that voluntary movement had the effect of reducing differentials in rates for comparable jobs, as economic theory assumes.

6. On the demand side of the labor market, there were certain barriers to movement of workers. During 1937–1939, employers had a "gentlemen's agreement" not to hire labor away from each other, and new workers were generally unemployed friends or relatives of present employees. The public employment service was used comparatively little by either workers or employers.

With rising employment which accompanied the defense and war boom between 1940 and 1942, some of these characteristics of labor mobility in a period of unemployment changed. There was a stronger tendency for workers to move from lower-wage to higher-wage firms, and the attraction of war plant jobs with better wages was overcoming the attachment of workers to neighborhood firms industries. The "gentlemen's agreement" on labor pirating was breaking down. In short, the rapid expansion of job opportunities at good wages was beginning to make the labor market behave the way in which economists have assumed it generally does behave.

FINDINGS AND IMPRESSIONS FROM THE SECOND STUDY [5]

Our second study, the impact of a textile mill shutdown, throws some further light on the character of labor mobility in a period of declining job opportunities. This study corroborated many of the findings of the earlier study and of the study by Reynolds and Shister to

[4] Distance has ordinarily been thought of as an important obstacle to mobility between geographical regions. Cf. H. Makower, J. Marshak, and H. W. Robinson, "Studies in the Mobility of Labour," *Oxford Economic Papers* 1, 2, and 4 (Oct. 1938), pp. 83–123; (May 1939), pp. 70–97; (Sept. 1940), pp. 29–62. Little mention has been made, however, of the importance of distance as a barrier even within a local labor market.

[5] Charles A. Myers and George P. Shultz, *The Dynamics of a Labor Market*, Prentice-Hall, New York, 1951.

which it was more directly related. Some of its principal conclusions are here summarized.

1. The workers who left their jobs voluntarily soon after the shutdown announcement were generally younger than those who were subsequently laid off. There were 60% under 30 years of age as compared to 29% of the layoff group in this age class. There were proportionately more men than women, and more single workers than married workers as compared with the layoff group. They also had shorter service at the mill, though the amount of seniority necessary for retaining a job was so great that this difference was not too important between the quit group and the layoff group. The characteristics of those who quit to find other jobs square with those of the workers who moved voluntarily in the 1937–1942 study.

2. Willingness to move voluntarily, however, did not seem to be a consequence of an earlier pattern of greater occupational, industry, or employer mobility. The workers who stayed on the job until they were laid off were just as likely to have moved around prior to their mill job as were the workers who quit after the shutdown announcement.

3. A majority of the displaced textile workers who found other jobs stayed in the textile industry, either locally or in near-by cities. These were the jobs which they were most likely to hear about and which they knew best. A sizable minority (around 40%) expressed a definite preference for jobs similar to those that they had in the mill, but an important explanation of why many workers stayed in textiles was that the job opportunities were best there.[6] Prior to their mill jobs, nearly two-thirds of the layoff group had made one or more industry changes, so that they were not people who had "always been in textiles" and knew no other work. After the shutdown, some workers found jobs in other manufacturing firms, but there was very little movement out of manufacturing. Again, this may be explained by the lack of good job opportunities, rather than solely by a decided preference for textile jobs or the inability to handle other types of work.[7]

[6] Half of the employed workers in the quit sample found other textile jobs, mainly in near-by cities in the fall of 1948 before the textile slump became general. Two-thirds of the workers who were laid off and found other jobs found them in the textile industry, but most of these were either rehired by the mill or by a new firm established in one building of the old mill, using the same equipment on essentially the same jobs.

[7] Cf. Gladys L. Palmer, "Mobility of Weavers in Three Textile Centers," *Quarterly Journal of Economics*, LV, May 1949, pp. 460–487.

4. Acquaintances and relatives working in the plant were the most frequent single source of information on available jobs, followed in importance by random application at plant employment offices. Comparatively few jobs were found through the state employment service or in response to newspaper ads. These methods of job finding did not differ from those prevalent in the labor market studied in 1937–1942 or in the study by Reynolds and Shister in 1947. Table 1 shows the

TABLE 1. COMPARISON OF HOW WORKERS FOUND NEW JOBS

	Present Study 1948–1949		Reynolds-Shister * 1947		Myers-Maclaurin † 1937–1942 %
	Sample I %	Sample II %	Sample I %	Sample II %	
Acquaintances or relatives working in plant	23	24	24	24	39
Random application at plant	21	14	20	42	33
Acquaintances or relatives not in plant	18	12	4	3	0
Employer solicitation	16	33	0	0	0
Advertisement	11	0	13	5	2
Returning to plant where he had previously worked	9	6	13	8	22
State and private employment offices	2	4	13	13	‡
Union	0	4	5	1	0
Other	0	3	8	4	4
	100	100	100	100	100

* Lloyd G. Reynolds and Joseph Shister, *Job Horizons*, Harper, New York, 1949, p. 39.

† Charles A. Myers and W. Rupert Maclaurin, *The Movement of Factory Workers*, The Technology Press, John Wiley & Sons, New York, 1943, p. 47.

‡ Less than 1%.

comparative findings of these three studies. Informal methods, in which the worker takes the initiative, seem well established in the pattern of job hunting.

5. A minority of workers had specific information about the jobs that they eventually took, frequently on rates of pay and physical characteristics of the jobs. But more frequently the displaced workers knew only that a certain plant was hiring or knew someone who worked there, without having any more specific information about the jobs open. The usual attitude was that "a job is a job" and "you can't be choosy nowadays."

6. Three-fourths of the workers who found jobs took the first job open without making any further search. Only a few actually turned

down jobs because of their physical characteristics, low wages, commuting problems, unsteady future, or lack of suitable living accommodations for out-of-town jobs. For the most part, therefore, there was little shopping around for jobs or weighing of alternatives, even by those workers who left the mill when jobs were still relatively plentiful. The same was true of worker experience in finding their first jobs or the mill jobs. These conclusions square completely with the Reynolds-Shister findings.

7. Willingness to move residence to another city for a job was confined largely to single workers, who had no family ties or responsibilities. However, there was an established pattern of commuting to the mill city from near-by cities, and, when the shutdown came, these commuters sometimes found other textile jobs in the area without having to change their residences. Most of those who were unwilling to commute long distances for work pointed to family responsibilities, particularly for small children, as limiting factors.

8. Displaced textile workers gave more weight to economic factors (such as wages, steadiness of employment, and chance for advancement) than to "human relations" factors (such as degree of independence and control, fairness of treatment, and relations with fellow workers)[8] in answering questions such as: "Why do you want to stay on (or leave) your present job?" or "Which are the best and poorest places in town to work and why?" The response varied with the kind of question asked, but in general it was clear that these workers who had lost their wage incomes and job security valued their recovery highly. When they had no job, the quality of human relations in industry apparently seemed less important than "a steady job at good wages."

SOME GENERALIZATIONS FROM BOTH STUDIES

These brief summaries of the principal findings of the two studies necessarily give an incomplete picture of the patterns of labor mobility that were found in these two local labor markets. The findings do not join at all points, for the methods and objectives were somewhat different. But certain conclusions are additive, especially when considered in the light of other studies of local labor markets.

First, it is clear that voluntary movement of workers is slight when job opportunities are few, as one might expect. Most of the mobility

[8] These factors in job satisfaction have been adapted from the Reynolds-Shister study, *Job Horizons*, pp. 6–7.

charted in the earlier study during 1937–1939 was forced by layoffs, and it was job-oriented rather than wage-oriented. The same was true of displaced textile workers in 1948–1949; they usually snapped up the first job they could find and seldom shopped around or made job and wage comparisons.

Second, wage differentials between jobs become more important in explaining labor mobility when there are rapidly expanding job opportunities, as in 1940–1942. The other barriers to mobility of labor also tend to break down during periods like this, when employers compete more actively for labor and workers appear to have wider knowledge of job opportunities.[9]

This tendency of workers to be attracted to high-wage firms when job opportunities are expanding rapidly is partially confirmed by the conclusion of the second study that unemployed workers value "economic" factors highest when they make job comparisons. These unemployed workers are still likely to take *any* job in a period of job scarcity, but, if they have their choice, there is a strong presumption that they will choose the one which is more attractive economically. The opportunity for such a choice is greatest when there are many alternative job openings, and this is more likely to be true when employment is rising rapidly (as in a recovery or national emergency period) than when it is at a stable high level, as in 1947.

The importance which displaced textile workers attached to "economic" factors in job satisfaction is not necessarily inconsistent with the apparently contrary findings of Reynolds and Shister on the relative importance of job satisfactions.[10] They found that workers (mostly employed workers) valued human relations factors first during a period of full employment in 1947. These workers, for the most part, already had steady jobs at good wages, and, in their scale of satisfactions, other things then loomed as more important to them. These findings, taken together with the material here presented, suggest the fallacy of attempting any universal generalizations on "what workers want in jobs." The answer will depend on what they already enjoy in their work,

---

[9] It is significant, however, that during a period when employment is at a high level but no longer rising (1947–1948), there is comparatively little voluntary movement. Reynolds and Shister found that the majority of employed workers do not continually make mental or actual comparisons with other jobs which may be available. "Workers who move deliberately from one job to a better job *which they know about in advance* are a minority of a minority—probably not more than 5% of the labor force even in good years." *Op. cit.*, p. 88.

[10] *Op. cit.*, pp. 33–34.

which is, in part, a function of the time dimension. In short, we can expect that changing business conditions (among other variables) will affect the relative importance that workers attach to various job satisfactions, and hence will affect their willingness to move from one job to another.

Parenthetically, it should be noted that employer policies which are concerned with wages as a means of attracting labor are more likely to square with workers' objectives in a period of rising employment than in a period when job opportunities are limited.

Third, labor mobility in the two periods of less-than-full employment (1937–1939 and 1948–1949) tended to be confined to neighborhood clusters of firms or sublabor markets composed of firms in the same type of industry. This tendency was more pronounced and more easily charted in the earlier study, for in the second study we had no way of measuring this specifically. But interviews with employers and workers in the second study showed clearly that a local labor market has segments or sublabor markets. Textile workers tended to stay in the textile industry, and nontextile employers, such as in foundries, were concerned with labor mobility principally in relation to other firms in their own industries. In many of those sublabor markets in 1948–1949, interfirm movement was confined to "hiring-in" jobs, which were largely unskilled. Union seniority rules and company promotion-from-within policies made it very difficult for an employed skilled shoe worker, for example, to find an equally skilled job in another local shoe firm.

Fourth, both studies point to the fact, also found by Reynolds and Shister,[11] that there is very little systematic search for jobs by workers, or weighing of job alternatives. When jobs are scarce, the average unemployed worker takes the first job that he can find. Jobs are usually secured through acquaintances or relatives, or by applying at various plant employment offices. Perhaps these methods of job finding could be characterized as "haphazard," although further reflection on this point suggests that this behavior appears to the worker as entirely rational. The worker's world is limited by his experiences and his contacts. When he loses a job, he turns to his friends for suggestions on where to look for work or he applies at the plants he happens to know about.

Fifth, the knowledge that most workers have of alternative job opportunities is limited.[12] Undoubtedly there is a small active fringe of workers who move around and know a good deal about conditions in

[11] *Op. cit.*, Ch. 6.
[12] Cf. Reynolds and Shister, *op. cit.*, pp. 46–48.

various plants, or at least they make the rounds of a number of plants in their search for work. But the majority take the first lead that they hear about when jobs are scarce. In the second study we found that many workers had very general impressions on the "best places" or "poorest places" to work in the community, but only a rapid expansion of job opportunities would have translated these impressions into movement of workers from "poor" firms to the "best" firms. Such a movement did occur during 1940–1942 in the first labor market studied.

Sixth, the fact that relatively few workers in either labor market in 1937–1939 or 1948–1949 found jobs through the more formal placement channels—the state employment service, active employer solicitation, or help wanted ads—emphasizes again the great informality characteristic of human contacts in the labor market during all but periods of rapid expansion of job opportunities. In normal times, the state employment service does not and probably should not function as the central clearing house for the labor market. A majority of workers do not use the service for job finding, partly because they believe that it has the least desirable jobs; and a majority of employers do not use it actively for recruiting because they believe that they can develop better work forces by their own methods or because they believe that the service has "only the least desirable workers" to refer for jobs. Employers, therefore, tend to file with the service their hard-to-fill jobs, and in some cases these are the least desirable ones.

These attitudes toward the employment service in normal times may dissolve in part as a labor market gets tighter and as employers find it impossible to get the workers they need through their normal recruitment channels. There was some evidence that this happened by 1942 in the first labor market studied.[13] In an emergency of national proportions, involving widespread manpower mobilization, the need for an effective public Employment Service is readily apparent. Yet its nonuse in normal times may weaken its effectiveness in periods when it is most needed.

LIMITATIONS AND UNANSWERED QUESTIONS

These two studies were designed to provide some definitive answers to questions about labor mobility in local labor markets. But their limitations deserve further examination, because they indicate the direction that future labor market research should take.

[13] Myers and Maclaurin, *op. cit.*, p. 49. See also E. Wight Bakke, *The Unemployed Worker*, Yale University Press, New Haven, 1940, pp. 249–250.

First, both studies were limited to manufacturing employment, and the second one was concentrated on displaced textile workers and where they went. We need to know more about the movement between manufacturing and nonmanufacturing employment and about the kinds of people whose mobility is largely confined to such industries as hotels and restaurants, personal service, and retail and wholesale trade. As manufacturing employment has expanded rapidly in periods of business recovery and national emergency, it has apparently drawn heavily on these sources of labor supply; but until recently we have no thorough studies of this type of labor mobility.[14] In short, broader analyses of patterns of movement in entire local labor markets are needed, yet this task is perhaps too great for a university staff with limited resources.[15]

Second, both communities studied were comparatively small, between thirty and fifty thousand in population. The Reynolds-Shister study was in a medium-sized city of some 350,000, and their findings did not differ materially from those in the smaller cities.[16] But extensive studies of the Philadelphia labor market, for example, indicate that in a large metropolitan area the wider variety of job opportunities available results in a different pattern of labor mobility. "Career framework" considerations, in which economic factors are very important, seem to explain many job changes in this type of labor market.[17] These tentative conclusions need further testing by research

[14] The first large-scale attempt to answer this question is the recent six-city *Survey of Occupational Mobility*, conducted by Cooperating University Research Centers and the Social Science Research Council for the U. S. Department of the Air Force and the U. S. Bureau of the Census (mimeographed, 1952). See the forthcoming volume by Gladys L. Palmer, *Labor Mobility in Six Cities*, Social Science Research Council, New York, 1954.

[15] For a discussion of some of the difficulties confronting labor market research workers, see Appendix A, "A Note on Method and Data," in Myers and Maclaurin, *op. cit.*, pp. 80–87; "Appendix: A Note on Methods," in Reynolds and Shister, *op. cit.*, pp. 96–102; and Dale Yoder and Donald G. Paterson, *Local Labor Market Research*, University of Minnesota Press, Minneapolis, 1949.

[16] The principal differences were, as we have seen, the different emphasis that workers put on economic job satisfactions, and also the fact that workers in the second study knew more about good places to work and poor places to work than workers apparently did in the medium-sized city which Reynolds and Shister studied. This suggests the obvious point that workers in a small community may have a wider knowledge of various job possibilities than in a larger community.

[17] See the essay by Gladys L. Palmer in this volume, "Interpreting Patterns of Labor Mobility," pp. 47–67. For a complete list of the Philadelphia labor market studies, see her footnote 1, p. 47.

which is co-ordinated and covers the same period of time in two or more different-sized communities.

Third, both of the studies reported in this essay are limited by their reference to the mobility of workers at particular periods of time. In the first study, the impact of changes in the economic environment over time was evident when employers were re-interviewed in 1942, but worker mobility data covered only the 1937–1939 period. Similarly, the work histories of the displaced textile workers were concentrated largely in 1948–1949, although some information was secured on their prior job experience. The Philadelphia labor market studies of 1936 stressed the analysis of job experience in preceding five- and ten-year periods, and even life-time experience. Economic considerations appeared to be more important in explaining mobility *over time*. We have seen that changed business conditions influenced worker behavior in 1942, as compared with 1937–1939 in the first study, and influenced worker attitudes toward job satisfactions in 1948–1949 as compared to Reynolds and Shister's findings in 1947–1948. More study is needed of patterns of worker mobility, and the reasons for it, over an *extended period of time* before we can say with finality that these patterns are either haphazard and accidental or the result of conscious career seeking by workers with economic motives paramount. The importance of such findings for public policy is emphasized by Gladys L. Palmer in her essay in this volume.

Finally, our two local labor market studies provide only limited information on the movement of workers into and out of the labor market. Of the 11,245 workers in the first study, 86% who did not have continuous employment in one firm during 1937–1939 "disappeared" from the records of firms representing 75% of manufacturing employment. Some of these people undoubtedly moved into nonmanufacturing jobs, but we did not know how many. A great many more were out of work for extended periods of time, and some undoubtedly withdrew from the labor market in the job-seeking sense. But how many left the labor market, and what was their subsequent experience? Research confined largely to manufacturing employment cannot answer this. In the second study of displaced textile workers, we found that the shutdown forced or induced about a third of the laid-off workers to leave the labor market. Is this what normally happens in a period of declining employment? What brings these people (or others) back into the labor market? Only studies over an extended period of time in particular labor markets will provide adequate answers to these questions.

5. Manpower Mobility: Two Studies

DALE YODER

Professor of Economics
Director of the Industrial
Relations Center
University of Minnesota

The two studies reported here were undertaken in the twin cities of Minneapolis and St. Paul by staff members of the University of Minnesota's Industrial Relations Center. They reflect a point of view toward manpower mobility that may well be made explicit at the outset. They assume that mobility is a quality of manpower that is of special significance in modern economies. The degree of such mobility is directly influential in its effects on the efficient use of manpower resources. Too little mobility can retard or prevent the effective allocation or distribution of manpower resources and thus occasion its under-utilization or waste. Too much mobility can have almost exactly the same detrimental influence on the application of manpower resources. Since human resources are scarce and valued above all others, their mobility thus becomes a matter of primary concern to all modern societies.

The mechanized economy introduced by the industrial revolution included many innovations, sharp changes from the long experience of mankind with earlier systems of production and distribution. It brought together large accumulations of capital or producers' goods in factories and mills; it stimulated vast improvements in transportation facilities on land and sea; it encouraged a trend toward urbanization; it inspired changing political and economic philosophies.

At least as important as these changes was that in which the new order instigated a system of large-scale work teams in which men participate on a voluntary basis. Both employers—the owners of capital—and employees—those who sold their services to such employers—left their comparative isolation in home workshops and manorial estates to move to one or another of these teams. What is especially important is the fact that these participants frequently left one team and joined another. They moved about; they changed jobs. Employees sold their services to a variety of employers. Employers hired employees as their services were needed. Sometimes wage earners could find no one with whom to effect a satisfactory sale; then they were unemployed. Sometimes they found no one who wished to employ the particular services they were accustomed to render; then they tried to change their tasks, to accept new assignments, and to perform other, different functions.

This arrangement represented a true revolution in employment relationships. Manpower that could and did change employers, jobs, and localities, that moved from unemployment into employment and out again—this new degree of manpower mobility was a phenomenon that had had no place in the long experience of the race.

The change by which mankind was "mobilized" was essential to the new employment requirements of an industrialized economy and became a major explanation of the vast increase in productivity. Mass production and lowered costs and prices created impressive demands for manpower. New products appeared in rapid succession. They could be provided only by moving manpower from former jobs and localities to newer situations. Living scales rose as manpower shifted from assignments in which compensation for its services was small to other jobs in which it was more valuable. Economic progress was facilitated by the ability of manpower to make such shifts—to undertake new assignments. On the other hand, immobilities in manpower and "frictions" that prevented its movement retarded effective allocation and utilization.

In modern society, these relationships between the mobility of manpower, on the one hand, and living scales and progress, on the other, are generally taken for granted. Flexibility, adaptability, and willingness to change locations and job assignments are widely recognized as qualities for which both individuals and societies receive premium compensation. The society whose manpower resources are adaptable and shiftable enjoys an obvious economic advantage. Measures that reduce such mobility—frictions in labor marketing and manpower allocation—may be costly to both the manpower involved and to society.

Mobility is thus in many respects the economically most significant characteristic of any labor force. It is closely related to and an essential factor in determining levels of employment, for the mobility of local labor force members exerts a powerful influence on both supplies of and demands for manpower. It facilitates adjustment of the labor force to changing demands for labor. A relatively mobile labor supply can and does take advantage of changes in demands; it adjusts its allocation to changing employment opportunities. A relatively immobile labor force cannot make these shifts so readily, promptly, or extensively. Accordingly, large portions of that force may be idle in spite of unfilled demands for manpower.

At the same time, known mobility of labor supplies influences demands for labor. The fact that manpower can fit itself to varying job requirements, that it is mobile, encourages a wider range of demands. New processes and whole new industries may enter a market known to have an unusually mobile labor force.

Similarly, the mobility of a labor force tends to improve the utilization of manpower resources. A mobile labor force is characterized by shifts in allocations to points at which effective utilization can be maximized. Employment is thus increased, and, at the same time, such employment involves higher levels of or more effective manpower utilization. The influence of mobility thus exerts a multiple impact toward improved application and long-term conservation of manpower resources. Waste of manpower is held at a minimum, because manpower is appropriately allocated in terms of its fuller utilization and because its unemployment or idleness is reduced.

On the other hand, manpower mobility can be so great as to permit excessive change and to impair optimum employment and utilization. If manpower is extremely mobile and if inadequate or inaccurate job information is provided, much change of jobs and localities may be misguided and wasteful. It may have undesirable social effects, disrupting family relationships, preventing political participation, and interfering with education.

Under such circumstances, interest in the extent or degree of mobility characteristic of local as well as national manpower resources appears thoroughly justified. A community may well be concerned with the presence or absence or relative degree of this characteristic in its local labor force. Whole regions—and the nation as a whole—have an interest in encouraging mobility on the part of their labor forces.

Mobility—the term as here applied to manpower is used as approximately synonymous with adaptability and implies qualities of flexibility, adjustability, and freedom of movement among labor markets—is thus a major consideration in the process of equating demands for and supplies of manpower. In addition, the influence of economic mobility has obvious and important social and political implications. For example, mobility is closely related to an open-class social system, in which men may move up the social ladder into preferred occupa-

tional strata. Mobility tends to reduce formal social stratification—
a condition that invites demagoguery in politics. Manpower mobility
has obvious implications for the "mobilization" of human resources in
wartime.

These assumptions with respect to the continuing social and individual significance of manpower mobility explain the effort to appraise
experience with labor mobility in Minneapolis and St. Paul. The
studies described here sought to discover measures of that mobility
as well as to indentify personal characteristics and other factors that
appear to have increased or reduced manpower mobility in these local
labor markets.

Factors in Manpower Mobility. What personal characteristics and
what institutional factors influence mobility? One means of finding
answers to this question seeks identification and measurement of existing mobility and discovery of such factors or circumstances as appear
to have increased or decreased these changes. Suggestions on these
points with respect to St. Paul had appeared in the 1941–1942 study of
employment and unemployment in that city. Important among the
causes of unemployment were a number of "labor market frictions,"
including inadequate and inaccurate information on available labor
supplies and job opportunities, inappropriate educational counseling
and guidance, restrictions on entrance to certain occupations, and
others.[1]

The later studies here reported reflected this earlier experience.
They began by asking what appear to be pertinent questions. What
are the facts as to mobility? What types of mobility may be distinguished and identified? What conditions appear to be related to varying degrees of mobility?

This report summarizes a few tentative answers to these questions,
answers suggested by two studies of mobility in local labor marketing
areas. Before consideration is given to what these studies show, however, it may be well to note what they do not and—because of the
nature of the studies—cannot show.

Mobility, as the term has been used in preceding paragraphs, refers
to the characteristics of individuals and groups. They are said to be
more or less mobile; they have more or less of this quality or of various
types of mobility. To assess the presence or absence or degree of such
an attribute, an ideal approach might seek to measure the quality
directly. In another approach, appropriate procedure might seek to

[1] See Dale Yoder, Donald G. Paterson, Herbert G. Heneman, and others, *Local
Labor Market Research,* University of Minnesota Press, Minneapolis, 1947.

identify circumstances in social, economic, and political situations that appear to facilitate expressions of mobility. Questions thus posed would include: How much or how well can this individual or can members of this group move into differing localities, job assignments, and employments? What personal qualities and what institutional facilities appear to aid or to hinder such movement? To secure answers to the first of these questions directly, some means of providing a clinical appraisal of the personal characteristics—aptitudes, abilities, interests, and experience of mobile and immobile persons—would be helpful.

Although some such clinical studies were included in the earlier St. Paul study, projects reported here make use of no such method. Rather, they represent only a preliminary step toward investigation at the level of a direct approach. They seek to discover what broad personal and institutional factors may be significant as affecting mobility. They approach this problem by analyzing evidence of the existence of mobility. They proceed on the premise that (1) if differentials in expressions of manpower mobility may be identified, then (2) perhaps the factors—personal and social—influencing these differentials may be inferred from a series of classifications of the persons involved.

Hence, in a very important sense, this is not a report on mobility as a personal or group characteristic, in spite of the fact that the data reported describe differing mobilities among various groups in the labor force. Rather, it is a report on mobility as a resultant—an effect, a condition presumably following from both personal and institutional factors in local labor markets.

This distinction is highly important in any attempt to understand mobility. From an economic viewpoint, for example, the evidence cited here must be recognized as reflecting not only the relative mobility of local manpower supplies but also the influence of local and "external" demands for manpower. Such mobility as is described could not have taken place if supplies were immobile; neither would it have appeared if demands had failed to develop or if institutional frameworks, customs, and conventions prevented movements. Moreover, in the presence of added and more diversified demands or greater freedom from institutional restraints, more mobility might have been manifest by the same manpower supplies.

Further, the type of evidence that can be secured at this preliminary stage in the study of manpower mobility necessarily fails to isolate the variety of social and institutional factors that may readily affect either (1) the expression of demands for manpower or (2) the expression of mobility on the part of labor force members. For example, if employers or employment services advertise their need for manpower, that publication of job opportunities may well be reflected in the actual changes that take place. Again, if local communities provide nursing homes for children, that condition may have a powerful influence on numbers of women who actually accept jobs.

Until the most important of these conditioning factors are clearly identified, the two concepts of mobility—mobility as labor force movement and mobility as the quality of being versatile, adaptable, and readily movable—should be sharply distinguished. As added understanding of actual movement is gained through more and better-planned studies, this distinction may become less important. The quality of mobility should become—as a result of such studies—more and more sharply identified with its quantification, its measurable degree.

This report describes labor force movement in quantitative terms—it reports what actually took place—and seeks to identify personal and group characteristics associated with these changes. On the basis of many such reports, it may be possible to identify mobility—the quality—and possibly to measure its significance in individuals and groups. From the accumulation of such studies, actual movement may be explained in terms of both demands and supplies, and significant characteristics of mobile supplies may become known and understood. When that level of understanding is reached, it may provide a demonstration that mobility represents a manageable approach to a realistic statement of the ancient law of variable proportions and more recent studies of cross-elasticities, which are at the heart of economic analysis.

Method of Analysis. The two studies whose results are reported here involve a group or "aggregative" analysis of mobility. They have sought, within local labor markets, to discover what groups or types of persons evidence greatest mobility. They have not gone beyond these classifications to discover why these distinctions appear.

The two studies represent an attempt, in part, to check the findings of the first study by a similar but more recent reinvestigation. At the same time, both studies seek to check on findings reported in other research. Further, the second study seeks to appraise certain techniques and methods used in these and other studies of mobility. The two studies differ from each other not only in time and place, but also in method. This latter difference deserves special explanation. The

St. Paul study sought to appraise mobility on the basis of evidence available from the earlier and more extensive investigation of local labor markets and labor marketing in St. Paul mentioned above. That earlier investigation was not designed to appraise mobility. Data collected and recorded do not answer several questions that would deserve a high priority in a special study of mobility.

The Minneapolis study, on the other hand, was undertaken for the specific purpose of appraising mobility and of testing several tools proposed for use in other more extensive mobility studies. It sought not only to compare evidence as to the existence of various types of mobilities but also to measure the dependability of several of the reporting techniques usually employed in such studies. More specifically, the Minneapolis investigation sought to secure evidence on the validity of information secured by interview, to check on the accuracy of statements as to reasons for changing jobs, wages, job assignments, and periods of employment. This study was also intended to evaluate the dependence that may properly be placed on the reporting of labor market participation and activity by non-labor-force members of households.

Both studies have been reported in detail.[2] They clearly reflect the point of view outlined in earlier paragraphs of this summary. They assume that manpower mobility as a process is the very center of economic activity and hence that qualities—both personal and institutional—that are associated with mobility are of great social importance. They seek, therefore, to secure indications as to what these qualities may be. To that end, they analyze evidence of mobility of several kinds and seek to identify groups with which these mobilities are associated.

Types of Mobility. Several types of mobility noted in these and other studies stand out clearly. Indeed, they are sufficiently distinctive so that one of the studies reported here describes what its authors have called "mobilities" rather than mobility. Unquestionably the most popularly recognized mobility is that generally described as *geographic* or *residential*. It refers to a movement from place to place. Second in popular recognition is probably *occupational mobility*, involving changes from one job or class of jobs to another, usually involving a variety of skills. Shifts from one industry to another are also important and are usually described as *industrial* mobility.

---

[2] See "Minnesota Manpower Mobilities," *Bulletin 10,* University of Minnesota, Industrial Relations Center, 1950.

These three types—geographic, occupational, and industrial mobility —are probably most widely recognized. In addition, however, changes of employers—without change of residence, occupation, or industry— may be noted. Similarly, changes in union affiliation may be regarded as evidencing mobility. Employer and union changes represent a sort of supplementary or secondary area of mobility. Perhaps more directly related to processes of allocation and utilization are movements into and out of the labor force and, to a lesser extent, changes from employment to unemployment and from unemployment to employment. Further, but not usually evident from studies of manpower mobilities, significant changes in jobs may occur without any change of employer.

The St. Paul Study. St. Paul findings are based on the continuing survey of employment, hours, and earnings of St. Paul labor force members which was maintained by the University of Minnesota Employment Stabilization Research Institute on a monthly basis from July, 1941, through June, 1942. Data were secured from a representative sample of approximately 800 households with 1200 members in the labor force (approximately 1% of all households and labor force participants). Data reported include employment status of all labor force members as well as their wages, earnings, and hours. Longitudinal case histories covering the 12 months were secured for one-half of this household sample. As noted, one phase of the earlier St. Paul study had sought to discover what were described as "frictions" in the labor markets of the community, thus providing an especially useful approach to mobility. (Special note should be made of the shortness of this period covered by the sampling survey. For this reason, authors of the report on mobility in St. Paul have described their results in terms of "short-run" mobilities, in contrast to the phenomena described in several other studies.)[3]

Mobility data have been secured by re-examining these household case histories after 7 years. Data show only what happened; the plan for the original study did not contemplate an investigation of mobility and hence did not seek answers to many of the questions presently suggested by various hypotheses advanced in connection with more recent mobility studies.

The Minneapolis Study. The Minneapolis study was undertaken in the spring and summer of 1949. It was planned as a pilot study

[3] For greater detail see Herbert G. Heneman, Jr., James L. Green, and Jack Stieber, "Differential Short-Run Mobilities, St. Paul, Minnesota," in *Bulletin 10*, University of Minnesota Industrial Relations Center, 1950.

to check techniques and tools as well as to provide information on hypotheses advanced by various earlier studies of mobility, including those of Palmer, Myers, Reynolds, and others. In addition, as an innovation, it sought to secure evidence on the possibility that various types of mobility might vary with economic status. A sample was drawn, for this purpose, on the basis of rental areas. Another innovation involved the attempt to identify "mobile" members of the labor force, on the theory that greatest attention might well be given to those who showed a high propensity to move.

The study sought information on mobility patterns for the most recent year and for the 5-year period just preceding the interviewing process.

In addition, the Minneapolis study sought to check on the limitations of techniques used in several earlier studies of mobility. The study investigated the accuracy of job-holders' reports on reasons for leaving jobs and for taking new jobs, on dates of employment, and on rates of pay and job assignments. The study further analyzed the accuracy of replies given by members of the household other than those actually employed with respect to numbers of jobs held and other conditions of employment.

Geographic or Residential Mobility. Of all types of mobility, local geographic mobility showed greatest statistical significance—in the sense that such changes were most frequent—in both cities. In St. Paul, 27% of the labor force changed residence in one year (1941–1942). In Minneapolis, in 1948–1949, almost 20% of the labor force made such changes. No clear-cut "mobile" type is, however, discernible on the basis of these studies. On the whole, males appeared to have a greater propensity to change residence than did females. Renters move more often than do homeowners. Heads of families were less likely to move than were other family members in the labor force. Mobility appears clearly to decline with increasing age. But differential rates of mobility based on varying economic status—as indicated by rental areas— appear to be unjustified by the findings in Minneapolis, where information on economic levels was secured.

Occupational Mobility. From several viewpoints, occupational mobility has greatest importance as indicating the flexibility and adaptability of any labor force. In St. Paul, 4% of the labor force changed major occupational classifications within the year. In Minneapolis, approximately the same proportion moved from one major occupational classification to another. On the basis of the two studies, greatest occupational mobility is found among males (this difference is slight, however) and in lower (20–24 year) age groups. The Minneapolis study suggests that the influence of educational experience is not prominent, for only slight differences in rates were found for those with wide variations in education experience and attainment.

Industrial Mobility. Changes from one major industrial classification to another were most important among those in younger age groups. Women made more frequent changes of industry than did men in Minneapolis. Increased educational experience seemed to have little significance, as did household income as defined by rental areas.

Entrance and Exit Mobility. Only the St. Paul study provides evidence on the characteristics associated with frequency of entrance to and exit from the labor force. Those who made most frequent changes of this kind were not clearly distinguishable on the basis of age. Women were more numerous among exits. Changes of this kind were more frequent among renters and among nonheads of families. These results clearly reflect the influence of selective service and expanding industrial activity in the national defense program in the period when St. Paul data were collected.

Reasons for Change. Several studies have sought to discover the reasons for job changes—as stated by those who moved from one locality, occupation, or industry to another. Records available from the earlier St. Paul studies did not provide information on this point. In the Minneapolis study, however, employees were asked for reasons. In addition, the reliability of their replies was checked by interviews with employers. According to those who reported the changes, two-thirds of them were made on the initiative of job holders. Most important reason given by those who quit was unsatisfactory working conditions. About one-seventh of those whose separation was voluntary reported "personal" reasons. Only 11% indicated wage considerations were a major factor in their leaving.

Checks with former employers resulted in agreement as to reasons for separations in 81.5% of all cases. That indicates rather high validity for this type of employee responses.

Validity of Reporting. Similar checks sought to discover the validity of reported wages, job assignments, and employment histories. In each case, facts secured from employers were compared with those reported by the employees who made the changes. Correlations were high—0.80 for wage rates and 0.90 for job content. Substantial agreement also appeared on details of work history dates.

Institutional Facilities. The Minneapolis study sought also to discover how employees found the jobs to which they moved. Several other studies have reported on these job-finding processes. In Minneapolis, hiring at the gate was most important in this function with services of a "friend" a close second. These results check closely with reports from earlier studies. Advertising, union action, and public and private employment services were lower on the list.

Significance of Wages. In Minneapolis, slightly more than half of all changes in jobs resulted in higher wage rates. The study was undertaken, however, in a period of rising prices and wages. Under these circumstances, the significance of wage increases as factors occasioning changes is not at all clear.

Household Reporting. One of the potentially most useful phases of the Minneapolis study is that in which it checked on the accuracy of reports on number of job changes. Such reports are frequently suggested as a means of screening and identifying "mobile" persons for further study. Evidence indicates that when reports are secured from members of the household other than the job holder, they tend seriously to underestimate numbers of jobs held. They underrate mobility.

General Conclusions. Conclusions from these studies must be regarded as highly tentative. The St. Paul study, because it was not designed specifically to measure mobility, provides less evidence on many significant points than does the investigation in Minneapolis. The latter, however, represents analysis of a small sample of the most mobile, rather than a cross section of the community.

These two studies do not substantiate many of the findings of earlier investigations as to personal characteristics that are associated with mobility. With respect to sex, education, and economic status, patterns of relationship—if any—are very indistinct. Only with respect to age is the evidence conclusive. It appears clearly that mobility declines with increasing age, although this relationship may be curvilinear. Institutional factors may account for an increase in job changes among older age groups.

Findings on reasons for change strongly suggest that respondents do not know precisely what occasioned the action. Certainly they did not take new jobs on the basis of stated reasons for leaving the preceding job.

Reports on means by which change is facilitated are consistent with earlier studies. Formal employment services apparently play only a small part. "Friends" and personal applications are more important aids.

Checks on the accuracy of reports from respondents with respect to job assignments, wages, and dates of employment are reassuring. Apparently, they can provide reliable information. On the other hand, the lack of dependability to be placed on the reports given by other members of a household creates serious procedural problems in all such studies.

6. The Balkanization of Labor Markets

CLARK KERR

Chancellor of the University of California (Berkeley) and Professor of Economics

Labor markets are more talked about than seen, for their dimensions most frequently are set by the unknown and, perhaps, mystic ideas in people's minds. A worker wishes to be employed in a certain area and at a certain type of job, and an employer wants employees drawn from certain groups and possessing certain characteristics. Unless it is said that each worker always has his own market area and each employer his,[1] there must be some adding of worker and employer preferences to get designated "markets."

These preferences vary from person to person and from time to time for the same person, and when they are totaled the "market" that they constitute has vague and varying contours but no ultimate limits short of those for American society itself. For example, there is said to be a market for waitresses in Oakland with certain women normally attached to it and certain employers hiring from it. Since, however, a woman need not always be a waitress once having been one and a woman never having been one can become one and since a restaurant employer can hire a girl from San Francisco as well as from Oakland,

---

[1] If this is said, then the term "market," with all it implies, might better be dropped. Instead, attention should be directed to the scales of preference of individual workers and individual employers. This approach might very well constitute a gain for realism and for precision but a loss for comprehension. It probably is true that no two people are alike, and for some purposes this is the relevant generalization; but it is also probably true that all people need to eat, and for other purposes this is the relevant generalization. The use of the term "labor market" implies that there is enough uniformity of behavior among certain workers and among certain employers to warrant generalizations about the actions of each as a group. Thus it might be said that the labor market for waitresses in Oakland is characterized (among other things) by sellers who want part-time employment and buyers who prefer married women, or by high turnover, or by a lack of formal structure.

the market is by no means a self-contained one with precise limits. Preferences of workers and employers are also relative to time. In a depression, a "waitress" may consider herself also available for work in a laundry, and a restaurant employer in wartime may be willing to hire former laundry workers to serve as waitresses.

Most labor markets are similarly indefinite in their specification of the sellers and the buyers. Such a labor market is merely an area, with indistinct geographical and occupational limits within which certain workers customarily seek to offer their services and certain employers to purchase them. But any single worker or any single employer may decide to go elsewhere. This might be identified as the "free choice" market or the "natural market," [2] for which the individual and changing preferences of workers and employers set the hazy limits.

THE INSTITUTIONAL MARKET

An increasing number of labor markets, however, are more specifically defined at any moment of time and have their dimensions less constantly changed over time. These are the "institutional markets." Their dimensions are set not by the whims of workers and employers but by rules, both formal and informal. These rules state which workers are preferred in the market or even which ones may operate in it at all, and which employers may or must buy in this market if they are to buy at all. Institutional rules take the place of individual preferences in setting the boundaries. Such institutional rules are established by employers' associations, by the informal understandings of employers among each other (the "gentlemen's agreement"), by companies when they set up their personnel policies, by trade unions, by collective agreements, and by actions of government. They contrast with the independent preferences of the individuals who are directly involved.

Economists once spoke of *the* labor market. Each worker competed with all other workers for jobs, and each employer with all other employers for workers. Cairnes, however, early saw there were noncompeting groups: [3]

No doubt the various ranks and classes fade into each other by imperceptible gradations, and individuals from all classes are constantly passing up or down; but while this is so, it is nevertheless true that the average work-

---

[2] See Clark Kerr, "Labor Markets: Their Character and Consequences," *Papers and Proceedings*, American Economic Association, May 1950.

[3] J. E. Cairnes, *Political Economy*, Harper, New York, 1874, pp. 67–68.

man, from whatever rank he be taken, finds his power of competition limited for practical purposes to a certain range of occupations, so that, however high the rates of remuneration in those which lie beyond may rise, he is excluded from sharing them. We are thus compelled to recognize the existence of non-competing industrial groups as a feature of our economy.

Cairnes used the word "compelled" advisedly. For the existence of "noncompeting" groups adds both complications to economic analysis and impediments to the maximization of welfare. Economic society would be both simpler to understand and closer to the economist's prescription if there were only one labor market.

In the long run, perhaps over several generations, it may be correct to talk about *the* labor market. Unless society has a hereditary class system, social mobility over time will permit, if not all, at least many individuals or their descendants to prepare themselves for any specific line of work. But a medical practitioner of today can hardly be said to be competing in the market with the unborn son of a pipe fitter. Yet in the long run, defined as the time it takes for the greatest occupational shift to work itself out, *the* labor market may be said to exist.

In the long run all families may compete with all other families, but in the short run most individuals are not in competition with each other. In fact, at any instant of time the standard case is one man faced by one job—this one job is available to only this one man, and this man has only this one job available to him. We are more concerned, however, with labor markets in the short run when several men and several jobs, rather than all men and all jobs or one man and one job, may face each other. In the short run a worker can make himself available for several jobs, according to his preferences, and an employer can make a job available to several workers, according to his preferences.

The noncompeting groups of Cairnes were the several socio-economic classes (manual, white-collar, professional workers, and so forth). We have found, however, that each of these classes is composed in turn of many largely noncompeting groups. Painters do not compete with bricklayers, or typists with accountants, or doctors with lawyers; nor individuals in Portland, Maine, with those in Portland, Oregon (except perhaps in certain professions). Barriers to movement are set up by the skill gaps between occupations and the distance gaps between locations. Beyond the specificity of skills and the money costs of physical transfer, lie such various but no less important impediments to competition as lack of knowledge, the job tastes of workers, their inertia and their desire for security, and the personal predilections of employers. The competitive market areas within which somewhat similar men look for somewhat similar jobs, and within which somewhat similar employers try to fill somewhat similar jobs, are normally quite restricted. It has even been suggested that the only meaningful definition of a labor market is one which calls each place of employment a separate market [4] and, perhaps, beyond that, each separate class of work at each such place. More commonly, it is said that a labor market covers the several employers in the same industry in the same area. Thus there are markets and submarkets, all more or less interrelated with each other. The introduction of institutional rules, as we shall see presently, generally creates a larger number of such markets and universally makes them less interrelated.

Institutional rules put added structure into labor markets. Lloyd Fisher has lucidly described the "structureless market" for harvest labor in California.[5] The characteristics of this market serve as a point of contrast for the market types to be described later. The structureless market, according to Fisher, has five conditions: (1) there are no unions with seniority and other rules, (2) the relation between the employee and the employer is a transitory, impersonal one, (3) the workers are unskilled, (4) payment is by unit of product, and (5) little capital or machinery is employed. The employer prefers one worker to another only if he accepts a lower piece rate and the worker one employer over another only if he will pay a higher piece rate. Rates vary greatly over time, but at any moment of time are uniform over space. There are no structural barriers to the mobility of workers and to the fluidity of rates. The only nexus is cash.

Structure is introduced into labor markets even without institutional rules. Many workers have skills which restrict the occupational area in which they seek work, and the number of these skills limits the supply to the employer. Moreover, workers and employers form attachments for each other which neither like to break lightly—"You must realize that the labor market is like the marriage market" [6]—and sep-

[4] "There are as many labor markets as there are employers of labor." (Gordon F. Bloom and Herbert R. Northrup, *Economics of Labor and Industrial Relations,* Blakiston, Philadelphia, 1950, p. 265.) Lloyd G. Reynolds states: "The firm is the hiring unit and . . . each company employment office is really a distinct market for labor." (*The Structure of Labor Markets,* Harper, New York, 1951, p. 42.)

[5] Lloyd H. Fisher, "The Harvest Labor Market in California," *Quarterly Journal of Economics,* Nov. 1951.

[6] Kenneth Boulding, *The Impact of the Union,* edited by David McCord Wright, Harcourt, Brace and Co., New York, 1951, p. 254.

aration is for cause only. Thus most jobs, even without institutional rules, belong to single workers or to small groups of workers. The craft exists without the craft union, and informal job ties exist without formal seniority rules. Institutional rules, however, add new rights and new preferences and strengthen the old ties.

Institutional labor markets create truly noncompeting groups. Markets are more specifically delimited, and entrance into them, movement within them, and exit from them more precisely defined. Such labor markets find their definition not in the composite of individual preferences but in precise rules. "Natural" frictions are replaced by institutional ones; the free and ignorant man by the exclusive and knowledgeable group. Market forces, seemingly impersonal in the aggregate but exceedingly personal in individual situations, give way to personnel rules which may seem exceedingly impersonal when applied to specific workers. Fraternity triumphs over liberty as "no trespassing" signs are posted in more and more job markets.

The sources of this enclosure movement are not far to seek. Employing units are larger, and bureaucratic rules take the place of individual judgments. These rules accept or reject classes of people, instead of the single individuals who met or failed to meet the tests of judgment or the prejudices of the small employer or the foreman. Workers have organized into unions which seek to establish sovereignty over a "job territory." Within this job territory work the citizens who belong to this private government; outside are the noncitizens without rights. The demands of all citizens will be met before the petitions of the aliens are considered. The institutionalization of labor markets is one aspect of the general trend from the atomistic to the pluralistic, and from the largely open to the partially closed society.

TYPES OF INSTITUTIONAL MARKETS

Many barriers divide the totality of employment relationships into more or less distinct compartments. These barriers have five sources: (1) the preferences of individual workers, (2) the preferences of individual employers, (3) the actions of the community of workers, (4) the actions of the community of employers, and (5) the actions of government. The controls on movement flowing from the last three are defined as institutional rules, whether they are written or merely understood, as compared with the "free choices" flowing from the first two.

The institutional rules of employers, workers, and government are enormously varied, reflecting as they do a diversity of environments and desires, and consequently it is difficult to generalize about them. There are, however, two general systems of rules, each with important subtypes. We shall discuss here only the two broad systems and not all the variations of each, significant as they are. The two systems are the communal-ownership approach of craft groups and the private-property method of industrial workers.

Communal Ownership. The craft union asserts proprietorship on behalf of its members over the jobs falling within a carefully defined occupational and geographical area. Employers needing the specified occupational skill in that area must hire union members or take the consequences. The building, printing, maritime, and teamster trades illustrate this type of arrangement.

Workers enter the market through the unions; and the unions have preferences just as do employers. They may be in favor of or against Negroes, or women, or students, or Communist party members, and these preferences will show up in the labor supply made available.[7] Entrance is sometimes through closely supervised apprenticeship systems [8] which require the worker to choose his specific occupation early in life and make initial sacrifices in order to gain admittance. These apprenticeship programs are usually pursued with government aid. Admission may also be by transfer card from another local. Occasionally, as in the case of the typographical workers, the man with a transfer card has equal rights with some local members. More frequently, however, he must go to the end of the list and wait until all local members are employed. The transfer card gives him preference only over new applicants for membership. When work is abnormally plentiful, some unions issue work permits, analogous to visas, which entitle outsiders to temporary employment. When employment returns to normal, they lose their privileges. They are renters, not owners.

Once fully in the market, the craft worker can move anywhere within it. Sometimes, when there is a hiring hall with rotation of

[7] Thus the "membership function" of the union, because of its restrictive preferences, may lie to the left of the "market-supply function." (See John T. Dunlop, *Wage Determination under Trade Unions*, The Macmillan Co., New York, 1944, p. 33.) The employer may also, however, because of his preferences, draw from less than the total supply of efficient workers potentially available to him.

[8] The classic discussion of apprenticeship, as of other union rules, is by Sumner H. Slichter, *Union Policies and Industrial Management*, Brookings Institution, Washington, 1941.

work, as for longshoremen on the Pacific Coast, he may move throughout the market. Inside the market, wages, working conditions, and job requirements are equalized, and the worker has an unusual knowledge of conditions and job opportunities. Sometimes worker performance is standardized also,[9] so that no employer need prefer any worker any more than any worker need prefer any employer. Though the men within the market are equal with each other, they are unequal with others outside the market. A little equalitarian island has been created in the midst of a sea of inequality.

Movement of workers is vitally affected. Occupational identification is unchanging and, largely because of this, other types of movement are encouraged—from one plant to another and even one industry or one locality to another. Since some fluidity is necessary in a progressive society, a tight tie to occupation forces a looser tie to employer, industry, and locality. Movement is primarily horizontal in the craft market. The worker gets his security not from the individual employer but from his skill, the competitive supply of which is controlled by his union; and he is known as a carpenter and not as an employee of a certain company. Just as the worker is free to move from employer to employer, so also are employers free to encourage such movement. "Gentlemen's agreements" against "pirating" are not the mark of the craft trades.

Ejection from the market is controlled by the union. An employer can discharge a man from a specific job but not from the market. Few discharge grievances are filed in craft markets because the man gets his security from union control of the market and not from the employer. The union, however, may eject a man, but its reasons are not normally the same as those actuating employers. Political sins are given a higher order of value as compared with the economic sins which an employer is more apt to punish. Union ejections, which are infrequent, are not so subject to appeal to third parties as are employer discharges.

The communal-ownership system is by no means an oddity. A check of contracts covering 350,000 workers in the San Francisco Bay area in all the major industries (construction, food and drink, retail, transportation equipment, wholesale, service, local transportation, metal and machinery, oil, chemicals, lumber and furniture, hotels and restaurants, public utilities, and others) showed 190,000 workers covered by some

[9] When it is not standardized, competition among workers is by degree of skill. The more skilled workers are in greater demand.

variant of the closed shop, i.e., membership in the union must precede employment. The San Francisco Bay area is, of course, strongly unionized and does not include a significant amount of heavy industry.

Private Property. In the industrial enterprise, the central rule is to each man one job and to each job one man. The typical market consists of one job for which one man is available. This is an exaggerated description of the average situation, for ability usually counts as well as seniority, but since the trend is toward strict seniority provisions it may stand as a statement of the central tendency. The man on the job (given good behavior) is the only man eligible for it, and when he leaves the next man on the seniority list (given minimum ability to perform the task) is the only eligible candidate. The market has been reduced to the irreducible minimum.

The production contract does not define the occupation. It sets forth the plant or company or industry. The plant or company or industry is the market. New workers are hired by the company,[10] not the union, but the union may impose its scale of preferences on the employer. It may, for example, refuse to accept Negroes or it may, alternatively, prohibit the employer from discriminating against Negroes. Bargained rules, however, usually first become operative once the employee is hired. The union then seeks to set a rising scale of jobs and a rising hierarchy of workers. As jobs open up, the workers move up in order; and as they close they move down in order. The worker temporarily laid off still holds his place on the seniority roster. For each job there is a worker and thus a whole series of submarkets where one job and one man are paired.

Two important qualifications must be entered here. First, many contracts do not provide for straight seniority but for some combination of seniority and ability. Jobs are posted and all men who claim the necessary qualifications may compete. But this is still an internal submarket to which persons outside the plant have little or no access. Second, usually there are several families of jobs—production, maintenance, sales, white-collar—each with a contact point with the outside world and with an internal hierarchy of men and jobs related to each other. These families of jobs constitute noncompeting classes within the plant.

The employer, and occasionally the union (for nonpayment of dues or some other offense against the union), can separate the man from

---

[10] For a study of employer hiring preferences, see E. William Noland and E. Wight Bakke, *Workers Wanted*, Harper, New York, 1949.

the market, usually subject to appeal to a third party. Institutional rules, set forth in a contract, often specify the proper causes for discharge—inefficiency, insubordination, and so forth.

The worker is held within this marketing apparatus not alone by prospects of advancement within the plant. He may be tied to it by a pension plan as well. More important, perhaps, is what would happen to him if he wished to leave. First of all, he would need to quit his job before finding another one since other employers, under the customary gentlemen's agreement against pirating, would be reluctant to hire him away from his firm; [11] and, second, in most cases, he would need to start again at the bottom of the seniority ladder in some other plant with lower status and income.

Movement, as in the craft case, is affected, but in a reverse fashion. Movement to another employer is greatly discouraged but change of occupation is almost automatic.[12] The important market for the worker is the internal plant market with its many submarkets spelled out in great detail. Movement is vertical in the plant instead of horizontal as in the craft market; and workers fight over seniority rights instead of unions over craft jurisdictions. The "haves" are separated from the "have-nots" not by a union card, but by a place on the seniority roster. When the "haves" compete among themselves, it is more in relation to the accumulation of seniority than in relation to the possession of skill.

Governmental policy supports both the communal-ownership and the private-property systems. Apprenticeship programs bolster the former; unemployment compensation rules, since they do not require an employee to leave his accustomed occupation or place of residence to accept work as a condition for the receipt of benefits, help hold workers available for openings in the same craft [13] or the same plant. These rules accept worker attachment to craft and to employer,[14] and

[11] For a discussion of the importance of "gentlemen's agreements" see Charles A. Myers and W. Rupert Maclaurin, *The Movement of Factory Workers*, The Technology Press and John Wiley & Sons, New York, 1943, p. 39.

[12] Most labor market studies find the worker's chief attachment is to his occupation, yet the essence of the seniority approach is to create an employee largely devoid of narrow occupational attachment.

[13] In some states, unemployed workers report to the union hiring hall to demonstrate their availability for work rather than to the employment service.

[14] A study in Nashua, New Hampshire, found, however, that many workers took lower-paid jobs in preference to staying on unemployment compensation. But this was a situation where a large plant had ceased operation and would not reopen. (Charles A. Myers and George P. Shultz, *Dynamics of a Labor Market*, Prentice-Hall, New York, 1951, p. 100.)

support a pool of workers in slack times into which the union or employer can dip.

Neither the craft nor the industrial institutional rules are completely new departures. Even without formal contracts, the craft worker holds to his craft, and the industrial worker to his plant. Employers hired craft workers for craft jobs and promoted from within before closed shops and seniority clauses tightened the rules. The institutional rules, however, do match men and jobs more precisely in the craft case, and the man and the job in the industrial case, than was done informally before their introduction.[15]

INSTITUTIONAL LABOR MARKETS IN OPERATION

Ports of Entry. Not all jobs are open at all times to all bidders except in the structureless market. Even in the absence of institutional rules, most employers consider a job not open for bid so long as the incumbent fills it satisfactorily; and employers generally prefer to promote from within to canvassing the outside market. Institutional rules, however, set sharper boundaries between the "internal" and "external" markets and define more precisely the points of entrance.[16] In the

[15] The case of the operating crafts in the railroad system is an interesting one, for it has elements of both the craft and industrial patterns. Normally, craft workers can obtain transfer cards, but production workers cannot transfer seniority from one plant to another. On the railroads, seniority rights are rigidly defined but employees do have the right to take their seniority to another location and "bump" less senior men there.

[16] Labor markets are of two broad types: (1) the structureless and (2) the structured. In the structureless market, there is no attachment except the wage between the worker and the employer. No worker has any claim on any job and no employer has any hold on any man. Structure enters the market when different treatment is accorded to the "ins" and to the "outs." In the structured market there always exists (1) the internal market and (2) the external market. The internal market may be the plant or the craft group, and preferment within it may be based on prejudice or merit or equality of opportunity or seniority or some combination of these. The external market consists of clusters of workers actively or passively available for new jobs lying within some meaningful geographical and occupational boundaries, and of the port or ports of entry which are open or are potentially open to them. It may happen that some such markets have only one port of entry, but this can hardly be the standard case as Northrup and Reynolds state (Northrup, *op. cit.*, p. 265, and Reynolds, *op. cit.*, p. 42). They may be right where certain large manufacturing plants are involved, but more commonly such a cluster of workers will face several ports of entry. The extreme cases would be (*a*) one worker facing one port of entry and (*b*) large numbers of workers facing a large number of ports of entry. The more structured the market, the more

craft case, the internal market is the area covered by the jurisdiction of the local union, and in the industrial case it is the individual plant. The port of entry in the former instance is the union office, and union membership (achieved through apprenticeship, transfer, or application) provides access to all the jobs on the inside. In the latter case, there are usually several ports of entry (each reached through the company personnel office)—common labor for production workers, lower clerical occupations for the white-collar workers, and junior posts for sales and executive personnel, among others—although if qualified candidates are not available almost any job on an *ad hoc* basis may be opened to outsiders.[17]   The external market is the totality of the labor force outside this one market or submarket, or at least that part of it which potentially might like to gain entry.

Thus the internal market has points of contact with the external market rather than interconnections all along the line-up of jobs. Workers inside the market, though they may compete with each other in a limited way, are not in direct competition with persons outside. Outside workers compete directly with each other, not with the inside workers, to gain admittance.

At these ports of entry, the individuals are selected who may enter. Employers have their hiring preferences which are usually dominant when it comes to hiring into the plant, although unions can and do affect these preferences; and the unions have theirs [18] which determine who gains access to the craft, although employers can and do affect them also.

The process of selection is also the process of rejection. Decisions are made in favor of certain individuals but at the same time against others. The individuals and groups which control these ports of entry greatly affect the distribution of opportunities in economic society. The rules that they follow determine how equitably opportunity is spread and the characteristics for which men are rewarded and for which they are penalized. The controlling individuals and groups may and do choose between prospective efficiency and prospective social

precise will be the rules on allocation of opportunity within the internal market and the fewer will be the ports of entry and the more rigid will be the requirements for admission. Institutional rules do not usually introduce structure into a market —it often arises from the individual preferences of workers and employers—but they uniformly add to it.

[17] Thus there are more ports of entry in a period of prosperity than in a period of depression.

[18] For a discussion of union preferences, see Clyde Summers, "Admission Policies of Labor Unions," *Quarterly Journal of Economics*, Nov. 1946.

acceptability. Since labor resources are being distributed, as well as individual opportunities, the comparative emphasis on efficiency and on acceptability affects the productivity of the economic system. When men fail to find jobs, it may be because there are not enough jobs to go around, or because they do not know about the jobs which do exist or do not think such jobs fit their expectations, or because they do not meet the specifications set by employers and unions. In the last case, as the specifications become more formal and cover more jobs, determination of the specifications becomes of increasing concern to persons in the external market who are universally unrepresented in the councils which set the specifications. For society to remain free and open, many ports of entry should exist and the immigration barriers should not hold outside the able and the willing.

Impact on Movement. One can only surmise how institutional rules affect latent mobility (the willingness and ability to move with given incentives),[19] but actual movement is, in totality, probably reduced.[20]

[19] For the distinction between "mobility" and "movement" see Clark Kerr, *Migration to the Seattle Labor Market Area, 1940–1942*, University of Washington Press, 1942, p. 151. ("Relatively immobile groups may move in large volume, and potentially mobile groups may remain stationary depending on the circumstances they face.")

[20] See Lloyd G. Reynolds and Joseph Shister, *Job Horizons*, Harper, New York, 1949, p. 48; and Lloyd G. Reynolds, *The Structure of Labor Markets*, pp. 55, 148, and 255. See also statement in Joseph Shister, "Labor Mobility: Some Institutional Aspects," *Proceedings, Industrial Relations Research Association*, 1950: "Union policies reduce the amount of voluntary mobility, on net balance." Other evidence, however, is exactly to the contrary. Lipset and Gordon conclude: "Union members appear to be more mobile both area- and job-wise than do non-unionists. . . ." (S. M. Lipset and Joan Gordon, "Mobility and Trade Union Membership," in R. Bendix and S. M. Lipset, *Class, Status and Power*, The Free Press, Glencoe, 1953, p. 498.) The two statements are, I think, reconcilable. Reynolds and Shister drew their conclusions from the New Haven labor market survey and Lipset and Gordon from the Oakland study. New Haven is a manufacturing town and most unionists there are probably covered by seniority rules which tie them to the individual plant. Oakland is a community of small shops and a distributive center, and most unionists are probably subject to craft rules which permit or even encourage them to move from employer to employer. The two studies come to opposite conclusions because they are based on observations of two contrasting situations. To be fully useful in determining the effect of unionism on mobility, two questions should have been asked or, if asked, then analyzed in both studies: (1) Did the worker belong to a craft or an industrial union? and (2) How does each type of movement (see the next following footnote) relate to union status? For certainly union membership affects both the number and the nature of the moves differently for the industrial unionist from the way it affects them for the craft unionist.

Whether the average union member moves less often than the non-union member, he certainly moves in a somewhat different direction following the formal channels set by the institutional rules. The craft worker moves horizontally in the craft area (Fig. 1*a*), and the industrial worker vertically in the seniority area (Fig. 1*b*). Interoccupational movement is reduced for the former and employer-to-employer movement for the latter. Thus they are both captives, albeit ones who surrendered voluntarily or even enthusiastically, of the rules which guide their working careers. Job rights protect but they also confine. Reduction of insecurity also brings reduction of independence.

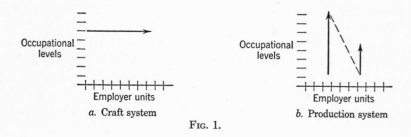

| *a*. Craft system | *b*. Production system |

Fig. 1.

Both craft and industrial workers probably have their geographical movements restricted, although some craft systems (such as specialized construction or typographical) force or permit great change of physical location, and some employers require reassignment from one location to another as the price of continued employment. Movement from industry to industry in the craft case may be greatly increased (maintenance workers) or greatly reduced (longshore workers); but in the industrial case it is always restricted. Change of employment status from employed to unemployed and back again is reduced in both cases, since both systems are designed to yield greater employment security; and changes from participation in the labor force to non-participation and back again are also minimized since both types of arrangements usually require a high degree of attachment to the work force if rights are to be preserved.[21]

[21] Movement of workers is of six types: (1) one occupation to another, (2) one employer to another, (3) one industry to another, (4) one area to another, (5) between employment and unemployment, and (6) into and out of the labor force. (A single move may, of course, combine several of these changes.) Craft rules generally reduce (1), (5), and (6) and usually also (3) and (4), but greatly increase (2); industrial rules generally reduce (2), (3), (5), and (6), and usually also (4), but increase (1).

Institutional rules affect the movement of unprotected workers also. Some jobs are never open to them, and others only under certain conditions. Also the fewer people who leave their jobs because they do not wish to forfeit their security, the fewer other people can leave theirs for there are fewer places to which they may go. The production worker is particularly affected. If he loses employment in one seniority area (he is discharged or the plant closes, for example), he must drop to the bottom of the list in the next area to which he gains admission (see Fig. 1b); or he may, of course, never get back into a seniority area (the case of the production worker who becomes a janitor). The more secure are the "ins," the greater the penalty for being an "out."

Competition among workers is reduced. The internal and external markets are joined only at restricted points; and within the internal market, craft jobs are likely to be fairly standardized and industrial jobs filled in accordance with seniority, so that workers are not actively contesting with each other for preference. Beyond this, the distribution of work opportunities by the craft union and the rehiring rights of the industrial contract tend to hold unemployed workers in a pool attached to the craft or plant and thus keep them from competing for jobs so actively elsewhere.[22]

All societies are stratified to a degree, although the degrees vary enormously, and a key element in any society is the character and the intensity of stratification. For our purposes here we shall designate three systems of organization: the "open," the "guild," and the "manorial." The pre-Cairnes classical version of the labor market was of the truly open type—all workers competed for all jobs all of the time. The guild system stratifies the labor force horizontally. Walter Galenson has described such a "closed labor market" under the control of craft unions as it operates in Denmark.[23] The manorial system places its emphasis not on skill but on attachment to the place of work and thus on vertical stratification. The industrial worker may demonstrate (albeit for somewhat different reasons) the same perpetual adherence

[22] The craft and industrial systems react quite differently to the impact of large-scale unemployment. The former is more likely to resort to some form of work-sharing and the latter to layoffs in order of seniority; the former responds to the claims of equal opportunity, the latter to a diminishing scale of property rights in the job.

[23] Walter Galenson, *The Danish System of Labor Relations*, Harvard University Press, 1952, pp. 195–200. See also remarks by Gladys Palmer on European labor markets in a paper presented to the Industrial Relations Research Association, May 1952.

to the plant as the serf did to the soil of the estate, although he does have opportunities for upward movement unknown to the serf.

The institutional rules we have been discussing move the labor force farther away from the open system of the classical economists which never, however, was as open as they thought it was or hoped it might be. But as it moves toward the guild and manorial systems, which will predominate? For they follow quite different principles of societal organization. The conflict in the United States evidences itself in the conflict between craft and industrial unions over the representation of skilled workers in industrial plants, in the effort of skilled workers in such plants to have their own job families and seniority lists, in the insistence of craft workers that their wages follow the market rather than the dictates of a job evaluation plan dedicated to internal consistency. In Denmark, the guild system is dominant; in Germany, with all the paternalistic devices of large employers and the life-long attachment of the worker to his plant, the manorial system, and this is one source of the union insistence on codirection at the plant level.

The stratification of the labor force affects the worker as citizen. Is he a free-roving mobile person ranging widely horizontally and vertically and probably having a middle-class outlook,[24] is he a carpenter, or is he a UAW-GM man? How he is located economically will affect his view of society and his personal identification with society and its constituent groups, and thus his political behavior.

Institutional Rules and Wage Setting. "Potential mobility," Hicks noted, "is the ultimate sanction for the interrelations of wage rates."[25] Other sanctions do exist and many times are the more important, but the less the potential mobility of workers the less the economic pressures that relate wage rates to each other. Institutional rules, to the extent that they reduce mobility, also lessen the economic pressures. As we have seen, some internal markets are quite isolated from their external markets by the working of these rules, and the interrelatedness of wage rates may be traced more to political, ethical, or operational than to labor market considerations. How do the rules we have been discussing impinge on the wage-setting process?

Extensive discussions with craft union leaders and the employers dealing with them in the San Francisco Bay area indicate that these unions do not generally use their control over the supply of labor to force up wage rates. They employ it rather to adjust supply to demand

---

[24] S. M. Lipset and Joan Gordon, *op. cit.*
[25] J. R. Hicks, *The Theory of Wages*, The Macmillan Co., New York, 1935, p. 79.

once the wage has been fixed.[26] If the supply falls too far short of demand, the employers are encouraged to introduce machinery or look to another craft for workers or even to non-union men. If the supply is too great, some union members are unemployed. This is politically uncomfortable for the union leaders and may require the members to undertake some work-sharing device. Further, employers may point to this unemployed group at the next wage negotiations and the members may be less willing to support wage demands with an effective strike threat. All in all, it is better to adjust supply to demand as closely as possible. This is done by controlling the flow of new members and by issuing work permits.

In neo-classical wage theory, supply (which is assumed to be relatively fixed in the short run) and demand are the independent variables which simultaneously determine the wage and the volume of employment. The standard craft market process runs instead along these lines: (1) the wage is set by collective bargaining in response to many considerations (including economic ones) and usually for a one-year duration; (2) demand which changes constantly determines the amount of employment at the fixed rate; and (3) supply is constantly adjusted by the union to keep close contact with the changing volume of jobs offered by the employers.[27] Control over supply is used more to preserve the integrity of the wage rate rather than to create it.[28] The wage rate determines supply more than supply the wage rate. Demand itself is subject to some control (foremen are limited in the work they may perform; one man may handle only so many machines; certain work must be reserved for a certain craft, and so forth). Demand, the wage rate, and supply all respond to more or less control by the bargaining institutions.

The production case is a different one. Industrial unions cannot control the supply of workers. Their attention is turned rather to stabilizing the demand for labor so that all workers with seniority

---

[26] "The jobs must be rationed among the seekers for jobs. And this is the important economic function which so-called restrictive practices play." (Milton Friedman in *Impact of the Union, op. cit.,* p. 213.)

[27] The supply curve may be shown as a straight line which stops at or shortly before the volume of jobs normally expected at the fixed wage rate. If demand moves to the right temporarily, the supply line can be temporarily extended by the issuance of work permits, which can be cancelled if it moves again back toward the left.

[28] This sets the craft groups apart from certain professional groups. These professional groups do not control the wage (the fee) and so they influence it by control of supply.

rights may have assured employment, for example, by introducing the guaranteed wage or heavy dismissal bonuses.[29]   These devices have no appeal to the craft unions.   But, for the industrial union, the supply of workers with seniority rights is fixed, and this makes it more conscious of the impact of fluctuating demand.   Institutional rules have two further wage results.   Since seniority ties workers to the plant, the industrial union must be more concerned with the effect of a negotiated wage rate on employment.   Were it not for seniority rules, wage rates probably could not have deteriorated comparatively so greatly for telegraph and railroad employees during the past quarter of a century.   The seniority tie to the industry has reduced the minimum price which would hold the workers in the industry.   Industrial unions, also, are more willing than are craft unions to make exceptions to the common rate to meet the necessities of the individual company and its employees.   Further, institutional rules by reducing the contact points with the external markets encourage formal or informal job evaluation plans as a means of setting rates acceptable in the internal market.

Under both systems of rules, wage rates are less effective in allocating labor (just as the movement of labor is less potent in setting wage rates) than they are in less structured labor markets.

The Locus of Control.   This reconstitution of labor markets reflects the shift in locus of control from the individual entrepreneur to the bureaucratic manager and to the work group.   And with this shift goes a change in values.   The entrepreneur felt personally the pressure for efficiency and expressed personally his prejudices, sometimes quite violent, about men.   The hired manager and the work group both respond more to considerations of security, of order, and of certainty—and, in the case of the craft group, of preservation of the all-around skilled worker.   By making men alike and jobs alike and placing each in a certain order, decisions are more or less automatically made by the rules rather than by individual men; [30] but these rules can reflect prejudice just as men in their actions can evidence it.   These prejudices may be the same (racial) or different (seniority, instead of merit), but

---

[29] Once the wage has been set, the craft union tries to adjust supply to demand; the industrial union, demand to supply.

[30] The rules are a method of settling the intense disputes between men over job preferment.   While the rules settle the individual disputes, they are themselves subject to dispute.   See, for example, Leonard R. Sayles, "Seniority: An Internal Union Problem," *Harvard Business Review*, Jan.–Feb. 1952.

prejudices, or perhaps better, value judgments, they remain. The rule of law is still the rule of men—once removed.

A further shift in locus of control may lie in the future. If the laws of the private governments of industry and labor fail by too great a margin to meet the definition of welfare as conceived by the public at large, then government may enter the labor market and try to impose its set of values. For example, in Denmark there is agitation against the closed labor market; and in the United States against discriminatory practices. The "planned labor market" may succeed the institutional market.[31]

CONCLUSION

Institutional rules in the labor market, as we have seen, establish more boundaries between labor markets and make them more specific and harder to cross. They define the points of competition, the groups which may compete, and the grounds on which they compete. The study of the import of these rules,[32] though less exciting than the examination of wage policies, is more needed. It is debatable whether wage policies of unions and employers have much impact on wage determination. It is not debatable that institutional rules in the labor market do have substantial effects on the performance of our economic system. These rules increasingly affect both the opportunities held open to workers and the contributions which they can make to the national product.

When private functional governments establish rules which so affect the unrepresented worker and the unrepresented consumer, the cry for public intervention is not long in being sounded even though it may not be very loud. Sir William Beveridge has called for "organized mobility" in the labor market,[33] as have others. This cannot be accomplished mainly as a consequence of guaranteeing full employment, as he claims, although full employment does reduce some barriers; for craft unions will want to control entrance to the craft, and industrial unions to provide for seniority rights, regardless of how full employment may be. Nor may the market be made much more fluid by other governmental actions. Seniority rules probably restrict the freedom of the worker and retard his efficiency more than the craft rules which

[31] See Kerr, "Labor Markets: Their Character and Consequences," *op. cit.*

[32] For a list of research suggestions see Gladys L. Palmer, *Research Planning Memorandum on Labor Mobility*, Social Science Research Council, 1947.

[33] William H. Beveridge, *Full Employment in a Free Society*, W. W. Norton, New York, 1944, p. 172.

are the customary target of criticism, yet government is not going to do much about them. At most, governmental policy can make more equitable the rules affecting entrance at those points of entry left open by the private agencies. Security will not be taken away from those who own the jobs, but nonowners can be placed on a more equal footing one against another in contesting for the vacancies.

7. Epilogue: Social Values in Labor Mobility

GLADYS L. PALMER

The general premise of this essay is that labor mobility has social values in times of both prosperity and depression and that it is essential to the proper functioning of the labor market in a semimobilization period.[1] Mobility provides the necessary flexibility in a labor force to meet changes in labor requirements in a labor market, an industry, or a plant. It gives the individual worker a wider variety of experience than is otherwise possible, and such experience has values to him, if his job disappears, if he has opportunity for advancement, or if for other reasons he wishes to change jobs. Although a factor in effective labor utilization under any conditions, the mobility of the experienced labor force is especially important in a mobilization emergency when the nation is dependent on the ability of its workers to change jobs or move to different locations to meet defense production requirements. In a period of semimobilization of indefinite duration, in which it is not feasible or desirable that man-power controls be invoked, the required changes must be met by voluntary shifts of workers.

It should be noted that, whereas there can be no mobility of labor without some turnover on jobs, there can occasionally be extensive turnover on jobs without much genuine mobility, in the sense of a major change of economic activity for the individual or a change in the distribution of employment in a labor market. This is because the ratio of gross to net changes in labor force status may be high and job shifts involving a change of employer only may outnumber other types of shifts. Occupational, industrial, and geographic shifts are usually more important for the dynamics of a labor market than changes of employer only or changes in labor force status only, and it is the

[1] Paper presented at the 1952 Spring meeting of the Industrial Relations Research Association.

111

former types of changes that are of major interest to a discussion of the social values of labor mobility.⌋

I am not unmindful of the fact that there are social costs as well as social gains in mobility, but I believe that in a free labor market the social costs of "too much" mobility can be more readily absorbed than the costs of "too little" mobility, and that freedom of movement itself has social values of great importance. I am not in a position to define precisely what constitutes "too much" or "too little" mobility in a given situation. Perhaps a more precise formulation can be derived when we have more information on mobility than is now available. On the basis largely of observation, supported by scattered bits of statistical evidence, I am prepared to make a subjective judgment to the effect that we had too much mobility in World War I, too little mobility during the thirties, and, without manpower controls, we probably would have had too much during World War II. Moreover, in my opinion, European labor markets have too little mobility to meet the requirements of post-war changes in the structure of employment in various parts of Europe. The general premise of this paper can best be illustrated by comparing European with American labor markets and by comparing the effects of mobility (or immobility) on the labor force at varying levels of employment.

European and American Labor Markets. European observers of the American labor market say that Americans have "jobs" but Europeans have "trades" or "professions." This characterization cannot be carried too far, since many American workers also have relatively strong attachments to occupations or types of work, but it epitomizes some of the basic differences in the labor markets of Western Europe and the United States. Relatively long periods of apprenticeship are required for many more types of occupations in Europe than here, as, for example, a requirement of 7 years for waiters or 3 years for booksellers. Relatively long apprenticeship training for a variety of occupations is perhaps more strongly entrenched in the Scandinavian countries, Holland, Belgium, and Germany than in some other parts of Europe, but is generally more prevalent abroad than here. In this country, mass production techniques have modified the skill requirements of jobs to a greater extent than in Europe. Moreover, in-plant and on-the-job training, shorter types of vocational school training, and promotion from related occupations have increasingly replaced formal apprenticeship, even for recruitment to the skilled crafts. For example, in a recent study of the work experience records for labor-force samples in 6 cities, it was found that four-fifths of the persons who had held jobs in the skilled crafts during the decade from 1940 to 1950 had had no formal apprenticeship training.

Vested interests in occupational training and experience tend to retard occupational shifts everywhere, but especially so in a labor market where most jobs require extensive formal training and the necessary certificates of training are a requirement for securing a job. For example, a relatively large number of unemployed young persons in Germany are literally sitting around waiting to secure a chance at apprenticeship training for low rates of pay. Again, the post-war labor market in the United Kingdom has been characterized by one English student as "an economy of few incentives and no mobility." [2]

With respect to geographic shifts, European workers are much less mobile than Americans. This difference is caused partly by serious housing shortages, as a result both of war destruction and of a low rate of new residential construction over several decades. Possibly, also, ties to a particular community have higher social values in Europe than in America. For whatever combination of reasons, the result is a low rate of geographic movement. Unemployed workers in the north of Belgium do not move to fill job openings in the south of Belgium. The refugee ("expellee") population in Germany tends to stay in the agricultural sections of certain provinces where there are too few job opportunities. One section of Italy can have practically full employment while other areas, at not too great a distance, have a persistently large volume of unemployment. In Sweden, there has been relatively high turnover on jobs but workers could not be secured in the industries and locations where they were most needed. Labor-supply problems have, in fact, been partially responsible for limitations of industrial expansion in Sweden in recent years. The immobility of labor in Europe, in some instances coexistent with pools of unemployment, has been significant enough to require special government investigations in several countries, and is of concern to all agencies working on the defense of Western Europe.

These points are stressed because it is my opinion that relatively extensive internal migration in this country has made for fuller employment and a more productive utilization of the American labor force. One element in the rising level of national productivity over past decades that is frequently overlooked is the willingness of American workers to move from less productive to more productive types of

[2] T. Wilson and P. W. S. Andrews, editors, *Oxford Studies in the Price Mechanism*, Clarendon Press, Oxford, 1951, p. 272.

economic activity. Such changes sometimes necessitate geographic shifts and sometimes not, but the combinations and permutations of occupational, industrial, and geographic mobility that are characteristic of the American labor market have been an important factor in maintaining and raising levels of productivity in the nation and in reducing extreme localization of unemployment, when major changes occurred in the structure of local employment. These social values are important to conserve.

Long-Term Trends in Rates of Mobility in the United States. It is generally agreed that the high rates of labor turnover and mobility which characterized the American labor market in World War I and the twenties have not been reached in subsequent decades.[3] Rates of mobility were low in the thirties when there was a large volume of involuntary job separations. Mobility reached higher levels in the 1940's but not so high as in World War I. These fluctuations suggest a downward trend in the over-all rate of mobility over recent decades, which is probably accounted for by the growing impact of a variety of institutional influences on several aspects of labor market behavior, including mobility. These influences were discussed in a paper by Shister at the annual meeting of the Industrial Relations Research Association in 1950[4] and need not be recapitulated here, except to note that various policies of management, labor unions, and the government, singly and in combination, have tended to retard the mobility of workers. To state the matter in another way, workers have greater equities in jobs in the fifties than they had in the forties or thirties and there may therefore be more resistance to movement in this than in earlier decades, under parallel conditions of business activity.

Generally high levels of mobility create more positive attitudes on the part of young people to the desirability of assuming risks in training for vocational careers and on the part of workers of all ages toward assuming risks in moving from one location to another or in shifting occupational or industrial attachments. During periods of relatively high rates of labor mobility, most job separations are voluntary, and substantial proportions of voluntary job shifts result in an improved earnings position for the workers concerned. In a depression, on the other hand, when rates of mobility are low, there is less opportunity

---

[3] Joseph Shister, *Labor Mobility: Some Institutional Aspects*, Reprint from Proceedings of Third Annual Meeting of Industrial Relations Research Association, 1950, pp. 12–14.

[4] *Ibid.*, pp. 14–18.

for variety of experience. When job changes occur, they frequently reflect downgrading of skill and many job separations involve relatively long periods of unemployment and the deterioration of skills.

The Importance of Mobility in a Semi-Mobilization Period. The task of officials currently concerned with manpower problems is admittedly complex. Enough mobility has to be engendered to provide a labor supply where it is needed for defense industries. On the other hand, too much mobility will tend to waste total manpower resources, and the latter are in sufficiently short supply to require careful use. The basic framework for required changes in manpower distribution is set by materials allocations and the award of defense contracts. Nevertheless, wage and price stabilization policies, unemployment insurance administrative regulations, seniority rules, and retirement pension provisions are not unrelated to the problem of effective utilization of manpower in the present emergency, since they influence incentives to the voluntary movement of labor.

The relative scarcity of total manpower resources in this decade arises from the fact that there are smaller labor reserves on which to draw than were available in World War II. This is because the age structure of the population has changed, as a result of low birth rates during the thirties and of other factors. Moreover, high marriage and birth rates during the forties have reduced the availability of married women for gainful employment in this decade. Job shifts by experienced persons currently in the labor force thus become the chief source of effectuating changes required in the structure of employment for defense purposes.

Despite a downward trend in rates of labor turnover over recent decades, typical metropolitan labor markets had a relatively high degree of flexibility for raising employment levels and effectuating major changes in the structure of employment during World War II and the post-war years. However, on the assumption that labor market conditions in this decade would parallel those of the latter half of the forties, several observers have forecast a further decline in the rates of turnover and mobility. If generally declining rates of mobility are in prospect, it should be emphasized that many of the institutional forces that retard labor mobility in Europe operate also in the American economy, although they are not bolstered by language or custom barriers and the indirect effects of greater social stratification of the population. It would be unfortunate, in my opinion, if what one European economist calls "an allergy to economic risk-taking" should spread among American workers as it has among European workers. The experience of this decade will provide a critical test of the relative strength of the social values attributed by workers to risk-taking versus economic security and also of the functioning of free labor markets in partially planned economic situations, both here and abroad.

Index